Epworth Comme

General Edi
Ivor H. Jon

Revelation

Epworth Commentaries

Already published

In preparation

REVELATION

Christopher Rowland

EPWORTH PRESS

Extracts from the Revised English Bible are © 1989
by the Delegates of the Oxford University Press and the
Syndics of the Cambridge University Press and are used
by permission

ISBN 0 7162 0493 2

First Published 1993
by Epworth Press
1 Central Buildings Westminster
London SW1H 9NR

Typeset by Regent Typesetting, London
Printed and bound in Great Britain by
Biddles Ltd, Guildford and King's Lynn

CONTENTS

To Catherine
Lucy
Thomas

GENERAL INTRODUCTION

The *Epworth Preacher's Commentaries* that Greville P. Lewis edited so successfully in the 1950s and 1960s having now served their turn, the Epworth Press has commissioned a team of distinguished academics who are also preachers and teachers to create a new series of commentaries that will serve the 1990s and beyond. We have seized the opportunity offered by the publication in 1989 of the Revised English Bible to use this very readable and scholarly version as the basis of our commentaries, and we are grateful to the Oxford and Cambridge University Presses for the requisite licence and for granting our authors pre-publication access. They will nevertheless be free to cite and discuss other translations wherever they think that these will illuminate the original text.

Just as the books that make up the Bible differ in their provenance and purpose, so our authors will necessarily differ in the structure and bearing of their commentaries. But they will all strive to get as close as possible to the intention of the original writers, expounding their texts in the light of the place, time, circumstances, and culture that gave them birth, and showing why each work was received by Jews and Christians into their respective Canons of Holy Scripture. They will seek to make full use of the dramatic advance in biblical scholarship world-wide but at the same time to explain technical terms in the language of the common reader, and to suggest ways in which Scripture can help towards the living of a Christian life today. They will endeavour to produce commentaries that can be used with confidence in ecumenical, multiracial, and multifaith situations, and not by scholars only but by preachers, teachers, students, church members, and anyone who wants to improve his or her understanding of the Bible.

Ivor H. Jones

PREFACE

The writing of any book is the product of a particular time and place amidst a network of human relationships and experiences. I am indebted to many people here in Britain and Brazil for inspiration, insight and support. It is impossible to list them all, but some in particular ways have assisted in the production of this commentary.

I am delighted that Kip Gresham has offered some of his work which makes a pictorial comment on the text. Over the last ten years we have shared much together as we have sought in our families to understand what Christian discipleship might mean at the end of the twentieth century. It is important for me that we have had this opportunity to reflect in a joint way on the mysteries of the Apocalypse. I much regret that financial constraints made it impossible to include more of his work on the Apocalypse. Janet Morley has allowed me to use some of her beautiful and challenging prayers from her collection *All Desires Known*. They perfectly encapsulate what I struggle to say in many more words. Sister Edmée of the Community of the Love of God shared her wisdom and support and agreed to let me use part of an unpublished talk she gave in Cambridge.

Ivor Jones in his typically kind and attentive way has assisted by his editorial widsom. I am glad that he was instrumental in suggesting that I write this commentary and grateful to him for the flexibility he allowed me in the way in which I approached my work. My friend James Penney read the typescript and made many helpful comments.

I have completed this at the end of twelve years in Cambridge. I have learnt much in that time from friends and colleagues, especially Morna Hooker who has been supportive of my explorations and a wise friend.

This book is dedicated to Catherine, Lucy and Thomas who have in their different ways assisted in the reflection which makes up this book: 'at present we see only puzzling reflections in a mirror, but one day we shall see face to face.'

THE PICTOGRAMS

The book of Revelation has produced powerful visions which artists through the generations have realised in different media. A classic example is Albrecht Dürer whose masterworks added breathtaking intensity to the text. On the central pages of this commentary are four modern pictograms by Kip Gresham, who shared with the author the experience of worship in Jesus College Chapel between 1982 and 1987. They are a selection from a series on the book of Revelation, 'a few seeds blown on the gale of this prophetic mind' based on chapters 6, 12, 17 and 21. Underlying textual themes like animals, elemental forces and numbers are captured in four plates, not so much in their mystical aspects as in a confusing roller-coaster of imagery, searching for patterns. The words of Revelation can create new realities, and drawings can give form and flesh to them.

INTRODUCTION

The book of Revelation presents peculiar problems for the biblical commentator. More than any other biblical book it asks us to suspend our judgement of normality and submit ourselves to be informed by the shock of what is unusual, for the sake of a better understanding of reality. I have set out to facilitate this process, which, I hope, explains, the kind of commentary that I have written.

A reader of a commentary might justifiably expect attention to the details of the text. The richness of exotic detail in a book like Revelation can easily prove so compelling that the panorama is lost to view. In a guide for preachers a sense of the overall direction of the message is important. Yet there is a risk that concentration on broader themes will lose touch with the text itself. I have decided to run the risk in the hope that what emerges will offer an introduction to Revelation. My purpose is to evoke interest as much as to explain, to persuade fellow-Christians of the value of this book as to elucidate with precision its detail. I am aware that Revelation opens the door to a world which most prefer not to enter. It is because I consider that this is a world which is worth entering that I have written the kind of commentary I have. I have not repeated material which is adequately dealt with in conventional commentaries. I have felt it necessary to include a larger amount of introductory material than might have been expected in a book of this length, in order to assist the process of understanding this very rich biblical book.

The task of writing a commentary involves reflection on the task of the exegete. The word exegesis has been conventionally understood as getting out of texts meaning which is waiting to be extracted, rather like pure gold which needs the techniques of the prospector. The text may then be read with understanding, and, for those reading from the perspective of faith, in ways which contribute to life.

Exegesis, of course, can be a complicated affair embracing the consideration of different manuscripts (no easy task, in the case of the New Testament, when there are hundreds of New Testament manuscripts which can lay claim to offer an authentic reading), language skills, knowledge of ancient history and culture, hermeneutics (the capacity to reflect critically and systematically on methods of interpretation) and analysis of the use made of texts. These are just a few of the disciplines about which an exegete will need to know something. Modern exegetical methods have tended to concentrate on the quest for the original meaning of the text – a quest which is one of the real contributions of modern critical interpretation. The scholarly endeavour over the last two hundred years has furthered our knowledge of the world from which the biblical writings emerged and the purposes they themselves were written to serve. But that is only a small part of the task of the exegete whose conviction it is that these texts in some sense can by their reading offer a word of life to the reader.

As preachers that is the essence of our task. We may not rest content with a historical exposition nor be satisfied with platitudinous advice loosely related to the text of scripture. A commentary for preachers can never be satisfied with ancient history. The collection of words making up the text to be studied are not really a veil behind which is to be discerned some greater reality concerning the world of the writer. All that is really important takes place *here and now* when the reader, in the midst of the contemporary struggles and perplexities, seeks to make sense of the text, in relation to the world and relationships with other people and with God. It is what the Spirit says to the churches *here and now* that matters. The word of life resides in that subtle and mysterious interplay between text, reader and our wider social and political reality. It is here that the Spirit acts; it is here particularly (though not exclusively) that we shall be able to hear the word of life. That will hardly ever be obvious and only infrequently compelling. Nevertheless it will often be surprising and challenging to our prejudices. I have endeavoured in this commentary to offer a reading which, I trust, is faithful to the text while espousing a view of its message which is contemporary in its religious and political implications.

The book of Revelation is not one on which I have preached a great deal, since most of my preaching takes place in the context of the Sunday eucharist in the Church of England – and Revelation makes only rare appearances in its lectionary. On the other hand it is precisely this book that has indirectly undergirded all my preaching and theology. Its appeal to the imagination, its challenge to the *status quo* and its evocation of a better world, all linked to a passionate concern for present responsibility, seem to me to embody those elements of the Christian gospel without which it ceases to be what it is meant to be: good news. And the good news is that things can be different because the impossible dream is a reality: the resurrection from the dead. It is a book which defies the precise definitions and constraints which our tidiness would demand.

The book of Revelation thus shows us that the world is no longer to be accepted as it is, that what passes for reality is to be unmasked and the frequent collusion of the world of 'common sense' with evil forces revealed. Its whole drama represents a struggle for wholeness, in which the separation between heaven and earth, God and humanity are at last overcome when God tabernacles with men and women. It is a book which engages with frustration and anger and owns them, in continuity with the Old Testament prophets, as potent forces in the lives of individuals and communities. Revelation has enabled me to be in touch with my anger, both about the Christian church, which, in its institutional aspect, seems at times to have ceased to hope that things can be different, and about the injustice and complacency I see around me and in which I know myself to be profoundly implicated. Revelation presents a mode of being and a model for action; it emboldens costly styles of faithfulness which involve taking risks (though not *any* risks) and standing up to be counted. It gives a licence to those who see the things of the Spirit less as comforting formulae or heart-warming exhortations than the challenge of the prophetic vision to which they are called to respond. Of course, dreams and visions have a bad press in religious history, yet without them there would often be no religious history to tell.

In John's account of Jesus' trial before Pilate, the dialogue reaches a climax with Jesus' assertion that he has come to bear witness to truth and that all who are on the side of truth hear his voice. Pilate's response is depressing: what is truth? The representative of the secular power confesses to perplexity about the nature of reality. At that moment John portrays him as being confronted by the criterion by which all truth should be judged. Jesus appears as a witness in Revelation and the necessity of witness is at the heart of the task of all those who seek to be faithful to God's perspective on the world. In its own very distinctive way the book of Revelation sets out to bear witness to the truth by setting forth its claim to be Jesus Christ's revelation of the way things are and will be. Of course, human claims

Introduction

to bear witness to the truth can be presumptuous, arrogant and destructive of community and consensus. Those who think they know it all can inflict their attitudes and certainties on those who are more tentative in ways which oppress and disfigure. Revelation's claim to reveal the truth may encourage this. Nevertheless it contains a timely reminder that there are times when it is necessary to recognize the difference between black and white and to assert with all humility that things are not as they should be and must not continue thus. In such circumstances the stand must be taken. The witness must by word and deed demonstrate that what is is not inevitably so. That task is costly. It is not surprising that witness (*martyria*) and martyrdom are closely linked. Those who bear witness have frequently found that they do it at great cost to themselves.

I am aware that martyrdom can end up being a very self-centred, almost pathological state, and also the way in which Revelation can encourage self-delusion and a narrow-minded vision of rectitude. Nevertheless, the dangers are equally strong of supposing that consensus, reconciliation and 'being all things to all people' are what constitute an appropriate Christian response. The problem with this apparently eminently reasonable approach is that it can end up with Christians baptizing the *status quo*. The present is left without any understanding of its shortcomings or any sense of direction which may lead to its betterment. Pastoral acceptability can make a vision of something alternative seem dangerous and subversive. Nevertheless the quest for inclusiveness can mean that the good news becomes protean as it seeks to retain acceptablity to the prevailing values and human interests. It is a point made very forcibly in a fiery document signed by church leaders in South Africa in the darkest days of the state of emergency. In the Kairos Document[1] they take issue not only with the use of theology to support injustice and oppression but also the theology of reconciliation which manages to avoid any significant denunciation and condemnation of injustice in the name of a bland concern for reconciliation.

Concentration on our own experience can readily lead us to assume that what is true for us *must* be true for others too. Of course, there are concerns of mine which run like a thread throughout the commentary. I presume, however, to have insights into the meaning of the text that are not incompatible with it, the rest of the canon and

[1] The Kairos Document, published in *Third World Theology*, Catholic Institute of International Relations 1985.

the understanding of the church's task down the ages. While it would be presumptuous for any one to claim to have spoken the last word on any matter relating to the interpretation of the Bible, there are elements in contemporary experiences which, I would want to argue, are true to the text and make some sense of the way in which the text can function (and has indeed functioned) in the mission of the church. This reading will question other approaches, though it can never exclude them. The recognition of a prejudiced reading should not be something to avoid, as I have attempted to suggest. It is necessary, however, to place that within a larger framework: first of all of the community of the people of God as a whole, past and present, and within the context of the canon as whole. I have isolated certain themes in Revelation which chime in with my experience and have enabled me to understand more of what it means to speak of God and to experience God in our world. Themes like exile, and marginality, the alternative values of the Kingdom of God, the positive side of the sectarian mind-set, and the need to pierce to the heart of things, to unmask reality. All these themes find their parallels elsewhere in both Old and New Testaments and so need not be merely the idiosyncratic insights of one individual. All of us who interpret scripture are having to oscillate between the part and the whole, text and context, and as a result are using models to help us make sense of that disparate collection of writings which make up the Bible. Whether it be covenant, salvation history, eschatology or salvation, all these guiding principles have to be used, tested and frequently regarded as incomplete guides. We need the guiding principle, however. In making sense of the details before us we are always using models which give some shape and coherence to the reality which confronts us while recognizing that there are always going to be loose threads which refuse to be woven into the fabric as a whole. The presence of the threads which stubbornly refuse to be incorporated into the neat tapestry of our world-view does not usually totally undermine that view.

The problem comes when that becomes an end in itself and we fail to take into account those parts of the tradition which do not fit with our prejudices. Thus, for example, those who are concerned to see liberation as a guiding principle will do well to remember that documents like the Pastoral Epistles do not fit so easily. The need for those of us who are more progressive to wrestle with such texts cannot mean a sacrifice of integrity. We are not permitted in wrestling with tradition to take short cuts either by consigning what we do not like to oblivion or subordinating our conscientious opinions to blind obedience to scriptural principle. We need to recognize the important demands that these texts make on us to take seriously the reality of our situation and the constraints which hem in the possibility of change, and the need at times for consolidation rather than change. The opposite danger is to be resisted of supposing that these represent the last word on church order and discipline. The book of Revelation has been the cause of the suspicion of those who regard its influence as deleterious of good order in the church. Its call to prophecy, martyrdom and pungent critique of contemporary political arrangements make it a text which is uncomfortable reading for those whose task is to promote the acceptable face of the Christian church to a suspicious world. In preaching the gospel of Jesus Christ, however, that dimension of challenge and the evocation of a better world are central to our evangelical task.

How do we read biblical texts?

We can expect the experts to provide us with a reasonably assured text and at least the basis of a translation, particularly if we cannot go back to the original language and provide that for ourselves. Let us not forget, however, that all translation involves interpretation. That applies just as much to making sense of the text in its ancient context as to making it applicable to today. It is essential, therefore, whether we be experts or interested Christian readers, to acknowledge the complex ways in which we find meaning in texts which are the cornerstone of our faith.

I want you to give some thought for a moment to the way in which you normally read biblical texts. Perhaps, in the main, you use notes to assist you in that process. Perhaps you come to a commentary looking for specific information about the meaning of particular words or phrases or the original situation for which the text was written, in order to provide an exposition of the text in the context of a sermon. We have every right to want answers which may satisfy our curiosity about the past. You may concentrate on the original meaning of the text as a relic of ancient religious literature. You may want to discover what the text might have meant and why it came to be written. You may be reading it as part of a house-group or Bible-study group in which general questions about the applicability of the text to your life may be raised. So, like Christians who form part of the Basic Christian Communities in Latin America, the concerns you bring to the text may be as important as the biblical text itself. You may, like them, be involved with your local community in a struggle: in their case for land or education. This may inform the reading. That perspective is one that deserves our consideration. Let us look a little more closely at this way of reading the biblical text.

Carlos Mesters, who has worked with peasants and urban shanty-town dwellers in Brazil for many years, points out that Brazilian biblical study grew weary of the growth of learned works on exegesis which had little appeal or relevance for the millions seeking to survive in situations of injustice and poverty. In that situation, however, a new way of reading the text has arisen, not solely among the exegetical élite of the seminaries and universities but at the grassroots.[2] Its emphasis is on the method: *see* (starting where one is with one's experience, which for the majority in Latin America means an experience of poverty), *judge* (understanding the reasons for that kind of existence and relating them to the story of the deliverance from oppression in the Bible) and *act* (constructive action for change in line with the gospel). Ordinary people have taken the Bible into their own hands and begun to read the word of God in the circumstances of their existence, but also in comparison with the stories of the people of God in other times and other places. Millions of men and women abandoned by government and, in the past, by the church, have discovered an ally in the story of the people of God in the scriptures.

This way of reflecting on scripture in the Basic Christian Communities is one in which story, experience and biblical reflection are intertwined with the community's life of sorrow and joy. That experience of celebration, worship, varied stories and recollections, in drama and festival is, according to Mesters, exactly what lies behind the written words of scripture itself. That is the written deposit which bears witness to the story of a people, oppressed, bewildered and longing for deliverance. While exegete, priest and religious may have their part to play in the life of the community, the reading is basically uninfluenced by excessive clericalism and individualistic piety. It is a reading which is emphatically communitarian, in which reflection on the story of a people can indeed lead to an appreciation of the *'sensus ecclesiae'* and a movement

---

[2] Carlos Mesters, *Defenseless Flower. A New Reading of the Bible*, Orbis Books 1989.

towards liberating action. So revelation is very much a present phenomenon: 'God speaks in the midst of the circumstances of today.' In contrast the vision of many is of a revelation that is entirely past, in the deposit of faith, something to be preserved, defended, transmitted to the people by its guardians.

So the Bible is for them not just about past history only. It is also a mirror to be held up to reflect the story of today and lend it a new perspective. Mesters argues that what is happening in this new way of reading the Bible is in fact a rediscovery of the patristic method of interpretation which stresses the priority of the spirit of the word rather than its letter. God speaks through life; but that word is one that is illuminated by the Bible: 'the principal objective of reading the Bible is not to interpret the Bible but to interpret life with the help of the Bible.' The popular reading of the Bible in Brazil is directed to contemporary practice and the transformation of a situation of injustice. That situation permits the poor to discover meaning which can so easily elude the technically better equipped exegete. So where you are, Mesters says, determines to a large extent what you read. This is a reading which does not pretend to be neutral and questions whether any other reading can claim that either. It is committed to the struggle of the poor for justice, and the resonances that are found in the biblical story suggest that the quest for the so-called 'objective' reading may itself be unfaithful to the commitments and partiality which the Bible itself demands. Mesters expresses the distinctive character of the reading he advocates in diagrammatic form:[3]

community: the context

|

Hearing the word of God today

The Bible: the text   Reality: the 'pre-text'

For Mesters, unless the real life situation of the people and the surrounding world are factors in reading the Bible, study of it can become escapist or entirely historicist in orientation and thus miss what the Spirit is saying to the churches. For ourselves, beset as we are by particular 'First World' problems which so preoccupy us, the issue must be whether our horizons are broad enough to include a

---

[3] Carlos Mesters, 'The use of the Bible in Christian communities of the Common People', in Norman Gottwald, *The Bible and Liberation, Political and Social Hermeneutics*, Orbis Books 1982, p. 122.

concern for those blighted by poverty and injustice. If they are not, we too shall miss what the Spirit is saying to the churches.

The threefold character of reading outlined by Mesters resonates with the New Testament itself. The scriptures that we interpret are an amalgam of story, legal precept, proverb, hymn and lament, epistle and apocalypse. That variety of literary expression and historical context should rightly make us wary of looking for one interpretative key, so that we construct a doctrinal edifice which encloses rather than opens the Bible to the totality of our existence. We would like the Bible to offer us clear guidance and its message to be completely transparent (see further on in the section 'Revelation and Certainty', 43ff. below), yet we may find that we are frustrated in our quest. All this raises questions about an appropriate approach to the Bible. The form in which we have the writings of the New Covenant gives us some hints about our method. There are three types of writing: *narrative* (gospels and Acts), *epistles*, (Hebrews should be included, though it more resembles a theological treatise than any other New Testament writing) and *apocalypse*. These facets represent three aspects of Christian experience.

The shape of the New Testament is governed by the fourfold story of Jesus. This is given its context both in terms of continuity and contrast with the Jewish tradition (particularly in the Hebrew Bible) of which this story is a part. The story, variegated as it is in its synoptic and Johannine forms, is historically particular while at the same time a foundation of our contemporary discipleship. The fourfold story stands at the beginning of the New Testament canon and its perspective constitutes the essential framework for the particular attempts at understanding what counts as faithfulness to Jesus. We are always going to be driven back to that story as the groundwork of faith and practice, not because of historical acccuracy but because for the community of faith it is the way in which the memory of Jesus is invoked, shared and wrestled with in the articulation of a contemporary faith. Nothing in the New Testament makes sense without this story. However much it may resist distillation and harmonization, it is that which compels our attention as we seek to give account of the faith that is in us. It may be protested that Paul's writings are chronologically prior and that he managed to have faith without apparently manifesting *any* interest in the career of Jesus. For us, however, faith in Christ *necessitates* that story and is inconceivable without it. The justification and character of Christian messianism is given shape by the gospels, not by the epistles.

The epistles' importance is that they offer evidence for the ongoing need for attention to our circumstances. They are a reminder of the contingent nature of faith and practice. Paul's letters breathe no sense of a rigid application of past norms to new circumstances. Far from it. A new situation has emerged: a non-Jewish setting and a (largely) non-Jewish people of God. Still there is the struggle to maintain continuity with the Jewish tradition and Christ. Indeed, imitation of Christ is one of Paul's goals (I Cor. 11.1). It may be that Paul does not need to tell or refer to the story of Jesus because it is presupposed throughout. Whatever the cause, the letters bear witness to a creative and realistic exploration of what faith may mean in situations removed from the particularity of Jesus' story. There lies the significance of the letters, not in the precise details of their faith and practice. They are binding on us in the sense that any human experience which claims to take God seriously demands our attention, particularly when it comes from those first communities who had the task of making the transition from their original setting while ensuring continuity. We may not like some of the solutions that the epistles come up with. It is their note of realism, however, which addresses the possible while attending to the hope in Christ which is so important.

The epistles must never supplant the gospels as the basis of faith and practice. There is a tendency to put gospels and epistles on the same level by supposing that the former were written for circumstances similar to those which provoked the writing of the latter. On the whole the gospels give us few hints about their origin and purpose. What they do present themselves as, however, is not occasional pieces, like the epistles, but authoritative pronouncements about the origin and content of the gospel (Mark), the career of Jesus as the humble Messiah (Matthew), the integrity of the Christian story (Luke) and the career of Jesus set in the context of God's eternal purposes (John). Local controversies may have provoked their writing (and over the years there has been a variety of suggestions about what these might have been), but the evangelists wrote narratives, not occasional letters, primary narratives, not theological treatises dealing explicitly with particular problems (as e.g. in I Cor. 8.1).

The book of Revelation stands on its own, though its contents are echoed elsewhere in the New Testament (e.g. Mark 13; Matt. 24-25; Luke 21 and II Thess. 2). No New Testament writing can claim to be apocalyptic in anything like the sense that Revelation can (Rev. 1.1).

Its closest parallels are with the revelation at Sinai for which affinities are claimed in 22.18 (cf. Deut. 4.2; 29.19), the revelations given to the prophets (e.g. I Kings 22; Isa. 6; Ezek. 1) and, of course, the book of Daniel. It appears to promise pronouncements which because of their status as revelation brook no dispute. More will be said later about this (see 'Revelation and Certainty'). Yet its enigmatic style prevents satisfaction of desire for the unambiguous statement. Its revelatory form contributes at least two things to our interpretative outlook. First and foremost, it confirms what has been stated directly and indirectly throughout the New Testament, that the fulfilment of the divine promise, anticipated in Jesus and in the activity of the Spirit, is the essential characteristic of Christianity. Secondly, its revelatory status refuses to accept the world as it is (see further the section 'The World of Apocalyptic'). It stands in contradiction to the view that the world as we see it is all that matters. Its emphasis on hope and the demand that reality, not appearances, should determine our judgement contributes a healthy critical scepticism about our circumstances. This can prevent compromise ending up in conformity and identification with the values of this age rather than with those of the age to come.

Thus the three types of New Testament writing contribute to our interpretative task in complementary ways. We need the perspective of each to prevent our being too wedded to the past, too tied to pragmatism and too starry-eyed about what is possible. Attention to what the Spirit is now saying to the churches, the stubborn nonconformity of protest, and vision to demand and pray for a better world – these are the themes of Revelation and its contribution to theology.

What is my/our story?

If we are going to seek to understand God's word, we need an honesty about ourselves, whether individually or corporately, in the particular situation in which we find ourselves. Such careful attention to who we are might seem to be a distraction from Bible study. I would suggest that it is an important way of bringing to our attention some of the factors which may well be unseen but nevertheless very real when we read the Bible and influence the kind of interpretation which we might favour.

When we read *anything*, usually something of ourselves is involved. I might go to a telephone directory in order to find a number or to a consumer advice magazine because I want to buy the best possible article. When I read a story about someone else, whether it is fictional or not, I will probably get involved. It may offer a distraction from daily life or resonate with my experience. Usually I don't give much thought to the emotions and memories that are engaged. To do so would be a laborious process when all I may want to do is to relax! I may resist the idea that I should always be too self-conscious about the way in which I read the Bible. It smacks of obsessiveness when I want escape from such rigours. I may go back to familiar passages for comfort and assurance, challenge and advice. Such moments of recreation in which my spirits are uplifted are necessary and hardly seem to need to be subjected to critical examination. Nevertheless with the Bible I am not just dealing with a book which is there to give me a relaxing time. The Bible is the primary source for putting me in touch with the ongoing story of God and the people of God in the past, present and future. If I want to understand something of what it meant for people to follow God and be disciples of Jesus of Nazareth, that must be my starting-place. However much there may be times that I would prefer matters to be different, I do not go to that book as if I were consulting a car maintenance manual, but as a varied collection of writings which reflect the different experiences of those who sought to articulate a faith in God and live by it. Its interpretation is never straightforward and its benefits come as the result of hard, patient and prayerful study.

When we read scripture we are doing so because we are wanting to explore how we can be better disciples of Jesus of Nazareth. Most Christians do not believe that they can go straight to the Bible to find answers to their questions. It is not so much because the Bible will not answer their questions (more often than not it cannot) but because, theologically, that is an inappropriate way of reading the Bible. Christianity has never claimed to be a religion of the book in which its tenets were set out in a clearly defined system of thought and action. If that had been the case, we might have expected Paul to have offered a carefully worked out system of theological and ethical teaching based on the words of Jesus. Paul does not do this. For him, and for most Christians since, the way in which one seeks to understand the mind of Christ in the present is a subtle blend of present experience and reflection on the story of God's people, particularly as it is found in the pages of scripture. Christians have talked about this as the relationship between the Spirit and the letter.

It is the present voice of the Spirit prompting us here and now, and the check of the past story of God's people, which produce an ongoing attempt to articulate Christian faith and action. It is a story which has no end. It is constantly developing and open to new insights as circumstances change and new challenges are met.

We read either as individuals or as a group with a story to tell about ourselves, our faith and our world. We come with particular concerns which will be peculiar to each one of us, reflecting our own psychological development and social context. Like the biblical writers, we have a story to tell, and our reading of them will need to recognize that. We cannot suppose that we can somehow put our experience on one side and, like empty vessels, fill ourselves with immediate answers from the Bible. We need to recognize the way in which who we are, and what dominates our minds and our thinking, conditions the ways in which we interpret passages. By so doing we shall be better able to identify the ways in which the wisdom of the past informs our circumstances.

If we do this, we have taken the first step towards a critical theology. It is the moment when we attempt to ask ourselves questions about why we read in a particular way, why our preferences are what they are and whether they might be different if our circumstances were different. We can do our criticism merely by asking questions about our theological presuppositions (i.e. is it my Methodism, Catholicism or Anglicanism which leads me to read a passage in a particular way?). It is just as important to ask questions about ourselves as social beings with a whole network of preferences, both social and political, which determine the way in which we approach scripture. We may feel that we are non-political beings or that religious and spiritual matters should be kept apart from political and economic matters. Of course, we who are reading the Bible do not actually ever do that. We read as people who are all the time making political choices and forming opinions about our world and the sort of society we prefer. Most of the time we do this unconsciously. We imbibe the prevailing opinions without too much questioning. Similarly, we can become part of a religious ethos and assume that this represents the totality of Christian faith and practice without being subjected to the broader horizons of faith and life which another tradition and another culture can offer.

It is helpful to us when we read any biblical book, but particularly one like Revelation where the opportunity for variety of interpretation and application is much greater, to read with heightened awareness of ourselves and our own concerns. At the same time we should keep an eye on the question of other readers' agenda too. In doing this we can appreciate two things. First and foremost, we can acknowledge that God is to be met in the contemporary story that we have to tell in as real a way as the meetings with the living God described in the pages of scripture. Secondly, we can have before us our immediate concerns, which may dominate our horizon because of the options that we have taken in life. Seeking to be honest about the second set of questions will enable us to be more attentive to the interpretations of those with whom we might immediately disagree, and also be as honest as we can be about the range of our prejudices.

There is always a risk that we will manipulate the text for our own ends. Nevertheless that risk applies just as much to the situation of the individual reader whose thought may be consciously guided by the expert whose notes comment on the text. More unseen, but equally pervasive, are going to be the welter of concerns and opinions about a variety of matters, religious, political and psychological, which are always in our mind as we read any text: who we are (our personal and psychological history) and where we are (do we read as members of an inner-city community or a wealthy suburb, in a prosperous part of the First World or as part of a Bible-study group in a poor shanty town of the Third World?). Recognizing what we most have to lose by taking the challenge of the text seriously, or what it is we might want to support or justify by reference to scripture, will help us to *hear* what the text says to us.

We can be helped in seeing some of our own concerns in reading the texts in particular ways if we read as part of a community. Part of the value of reading a text together is that it is going to give us an opportunity to share our opinions and have them modified or at least put alongside others. Most important of all, if we read as part of a Christian community, we shall be guided in our reading by the general guidance of Christians down the centuries who have worked out ways in which we can make sense of the biblical message. Those guidelines will not be narrow and restricting but enable us to remember that the story we are reading about does have some shape and has an overall coherence about it.

Here too caution is necessary, however. The wider setting of the life of the individual or group is a fallen and fragmented world, and that small group is part of a wider church. The scriptures and their interpretation are not just *our* business (when ours is conceived in terms only of a narrow interest-group). That group is a collection of individuals with differing concerns, conscious or unconscious, and personalities. Tendency to dominate can inhibit the contributions of weaker or more reticent members and so the triumph of one line of interpretation. Despite this caveat, that communal dimension of biblical reflection can inform, clarify and allow the work of the Spirit whose dwelling is in the body of believers as a whole (I Cor. 12).

In important respects the book of Revelation coincides with this approach to scripture. Despite its concern with the fulfilment of God's purposes, it is is very much rooted in the present practice of men and women at a particular time and place. Its dominant concern is what the Spirit says to the churches. That involves them in the obligation to explore to the full the character of that situation in which they find themselves. They are asked to understand the truth about their standing before God, and also the nature of the institutions which confront them and the reality of the struggle of which they are a part. Some might not perceive it, others might be aware of it and at the point of giving up. The insight into the reality of what may be going on, and an appropriate response, are common factors linking the theology of liberation as outlined by Carlos Mesters and the message of the book of Revelation.

The external circumstances of life in Western Europe are of the apparent triumph of liberal capitalism. The euphoria which attends the demise of socialism and related communitarian and internationalist projects poses problems of a very specific kind for the Christian interpreter. Our foundation documents are replete with repudiation of that commodity which is the particular idol of our age: Mammon. In such circumstances those who find themselves adjusting with difficulty to the prevailing culture, and indeed whose inner life is to an extent formed in reaction to it by developing strategies of coping and survival, can often be at a loss as to how to act. Appeals to those characteristics of weakness, self-effacement, intuition, feeling and co-operation sit uneasily with a rampant individualism, 'machismo' and self-promotion. It is not difficult to see the attraction of a book whose *strength* lies in the promotion of a symbol of defeat and weakness (Rev. 5) and which recognizes the importance of power but offers a very different perspective as to its exercise.

We are complicated beings who do not readily conform to patterns. The very wealth and variety of human experience will make us diffident about generalizing about what it is we might find in a text. Nevertheless a process of identifying who we are will go some way towards enabling us to understanding why the beast we may identify in our lives may take the form it does, and, in the midst of the welter of advice from the Risen Christ to the churches, whether we need the gentle support for the persecuted and oppressed or the stern rebuke for complacent and wealthy Christians.

The world of Revelation

We have concentrated so far on ourselves, our own prejudices and concerns as an indispensable part of understanding how and why we read as we do. However important that awareness of the present may be, we need to remember that we are reading a text produced in a very different culture from our own. We have to understand something of the text we are reading and its nature and purpose. Of course, we are rarely in the position of being able to determine the answers to these questions with any degree of certainty and so must depend on filling in the bits of the jigsaw from the various pieces given to us in the text itself. The task of doing this can, however, remind us that this text was written and read at another time and another place by people in very different circumstances from ourselves. Our interpretation of the images of Revelation cannot be the last word on the subject.

Revelation reminds us more keenly than most New Testament documents that it belongs to another age and culture. Its thought forms and language seems so far removed from our own. While much of this commentary will not be attempting to reconstruct what the text might have meant to Christians in Asia Minor, it is necessary to remember that it was written to particular people at a particular time and place. The letters to the angels of the seven churches in chs. 2 and 3 show its setting in and some knowledge of the Christian communities in seven cities in Asia Minor (modern Turkey). John is in exile, and it is in that situation that he records his vision of the apocalypse (revelation) of Jesus Christ (1.1). The situation confronting the churches is not uniformly one of persecution (the fate of Antipas in 2.13 is an exception). The church in Smyrna seems to have been undergoing harassment from the Jewish synagogue (2.9; 3.9). Elsewhere, the issues seem to be more concerned with maintaining the distinctive identity of Christian discipleship in the face of temptations to merge with surrounding society.

Traditionally the date has been towards the end of the reign of the Emperor Domitian (the mid-nineties), who took action against some members of the imperial household for their atheism (that may be a reference to Christianity but equally have been Judaism).[4] That may have been part of a much wider attempt to extract a tax from Jews and sympathizers (Christians would have fallen into that category). In that situation there may have been a wave of sporadic persecution, but there is uncertainty whether it was on the empire-wide scope of earlier persecutions. Evidence from Revelation itself suggests that an earlier date is equally likely. This derives from the most obvious reading of Rev. 17.9f. If we identify the kings with the first five Roman emperors (Augustus, Tiberius, Caligula, Claudius, Nero), that would lead us to suppose that Nero is the last of the five whose return from death may be hinted at in 17.11 (this was a widespread rumour at the end of the first century). After Nero's death in 68 there were four claimants to the office in a year (Galba, Otho, Vitellius and Vespasian, who finally became emperor). So it was during the period of great upheaval in the empire while the power struggle was going on that John saw his vision. The connection with Nero would be supported if the cryptic reference to the number of the beast in 13.18 is the numerical value of Nero Caesar in Hebrew: $n = 50$, $r = 200$, $w = 6$, $q = 100$, $s = 60$, so NRWN QSR = 666. A similar kind of numerical game was often employed in contemporary Jewish works, e.g. the *Sibylline Oracles* I 324ff.[5]

The world of apocalyptic

In the discussion of apocalyptic in the last thirty years or so, there has been a significant difference of opinion about its origins. Two accounts of its background call for some consideration, as they demonstrate the way in which assumptions are made about its character and place in the biblical tradition.

On the one hand (and this view is the majority opinion at present) there are those who consider that apocalyptic is the successor to the prophetic movement, and particularly to the future of hope of the prophets. The concern with human history and the vindication of Israel's hopes is said to represent the formulation of the prophetic hope in the changed circumstances of another age.

This point of view has been very influential, because it has seemed

---

[4] See the Roman historian Dio Cassius, *Histories* 67.14.
[5] There is a discussion of the identification by the second-century Christian writer Irenaeus in his book *Against the Heresies* V 30. 3.

to many that in the apocalyptic literature written round about the beginning of the Christian era, the future hope dominates even if it has been placed on a supernatural plane. Its stress, it is suggested, is on the supernatural and other-worldly, just as in Revelation 21 the seer looks forward to a new heaven and new earth with the old creation having passed away. While this view has been most influential, it has not gone unchallenged. It has been suggested that it is the Wisdom tradition of the Old Testament with its interest in understanding the cosmos and the ways of the world which was the real antecedent of apocalyptic and not the prophetic movement. The distinguished German interpreter, Gerhard von Rad, in his *Old Testament Theology*[6] argued that it is in the Wisdom tradition that we must look for the origin of apocalyptic. He noted some points of contact between the apocalypses and the Wisdom books, particularly the fact that apocalyptic is concerned with knowledge, not only of the age to come but also of things in heaven and the mysteries of human existence. Such a preoccupation seems to be akin to features of the Wisdom literature (particularly the book of Job). The activities of certain wise men in antiquity were not at all dissimilar from the concerns of the writers of the apocalypses. There is some trace of the role of such figures in the Old Testament, e.g. in the Joseph stories in Genesis, but particularly in the stories about Daniel, the Jewish seer who interprets the dreams of Nebuchadnezzar and is regarded as a sage superior to all those in the king's court. Dreams, visions, and the like are all typical features of the apocalypses, and it is now recognized that this may indeed provide an important contribution to our understanding of the apocalyptic tradition of which Revelation is a part. It will be seen how very different these two approaches to apocalyptic are: on the one hand we have a description of it as a phenomenon whose primary concern is with the future, derived from the prophetic hope, and on the other we find an account of it which concentrates on its quest for knowledge in its totality, of which interest in the future is only a part, however significant. We probably do not have to choose between them but can recognize how both may shed light on Revelation.

We can understand the disparate elements of the book of Revelation, however, if we see the underlying theme to be one which derives from its initial statement 'The Revelation of Jesus Christ' (Rev. 1.1). Revelation is not merely an eschatological tract satisfying

[6] G. von Rad, *Old Testament Theology* I–II, ET Oliver and Boyd 1962, 1965.

the curiosity of those who wanted to know what would happen in the future. Its purpose is to reveal something hidden which will enable the readers to view their present situation from a completely different perspective, that of the Risen Christ. When seen in this light, the significance of many of the visions in the Apocalypse fall into place: the letters to the churches offer an assessment of their churches' worth from a divine perspective; the vision of the divine throne-room in Revelation 4 enables the churches to recognize the dominion of their God; in Revelation 5, the death and exaltation of Christ is shown to mark the inauguration of the new age; and in chs. 13 and 17 the true identity of the State is divulged. Revelation is a text which seeks to summon to repentance and to give reassurance by showing – by means of direct revelation from God – that there is a divine dimension to material existence, which could be, and was being, ignored by the churches of Asia Minor.

Looking at it in this light, we can begin to see why Martin Hengel should have suggested that apocalyptic might be better understood as part of a much wider religious phenomenon in late antiquity: what he called 'higher wisdom by revelation'.[7] He points to many parallels between the quest for knowledge through revelation in the apocalypses and non-Jewish material, as well as stressing the widespread trend in antiquity towards the irrational and the mysterious, so that revelation of what was hidden with God became an indispensable means of giving meaning and purpose to human existence.

If we think of apocalyptic in this way, we shall be able to see how the claim of the Jewish apocalypses, written at roughly the same time as Revelation, to reveal mysteries about the future, the movements of the stars, the heavenly dwelling of God, angelology, the course of human history and the mystery of the human plight *all* fall within the category of the mysteries which can only be solved by higher wisdom through revelation. Such a quest makes sense of the piety manifested in the apocalypses. Indeed, the impact of the message of Revelation depends very much on its claim to be a direct revelation from heaven, rather than the mere opinion of humankind.

Apocalyptic thus offers its readers an answer to that heartfelt plea from the prophet in Isaiah 64.1: 'Why did you not tear asunder the heavens and come down?' Many in John's day would have echoed the question of oppressed Jews of a previous generation: 'Where is your zeal, your valour, your burning and tender love? Do not stand

---

[7] M. Hengel, *Judaism and Hellenism*, ET SCM Press 1974, vol. I p. 217.

aloof' (Isa. 63.15). An apocalypse offered a basis for hope in a world where God seemed to be restrained, by unmasking the reality of what the past, the present and the future of human history were actually about. The apocalyptic unveiling reveals that the future triumph of the divine righteousnesss is assured. One of the functions of an apocalypse is to provoke a response of identification with the divine purposes by the individual or community in view of the inevitable outcome of the triumph of God. Apocalyptic visions offer a hope of a better world which shows up the inadequacy of the present. As such they were an important part of creating a critical outlook on the world order and promoting a distance from the fabric of society as presently constituted. The injustice in the world and the temporary nature of the present order are demonstrated as a spur of action in pursuit of the goal of the reign of God.

In an apocalypse what happens in heaven corresponds to what happens on earth. It is a kind of overview from another perspective. It is not as if John is offered a photographic representation of reality, past, present and future. The relationship between the symbol used and the human perception is more indirect, and yet because of its many facets more suggestive about the reality which it seeks to convey. The language which Jewish tradition used to speak of God's mysteries is in Revelation evoked to enable the reader to understand the consequences of Christ's brutal death better than would be possible in a mere narrative. It is that which is the focal point of John's vision. The perspective offered to John shows little concern with history before Jesus. Rather it is that life which is presented as the key to the purposes of God and the meaning of history.

Revelation is not mere prediction. Of course, it speaks about the future, but it is a future (and a present) viewed in the light of the God who now reigns and will be seen to reign on earth. John is commissioned to write 'what is now, and what is to take place hereafter' (Rev. 1.19). It is like a drama happening on two levels in which the 'higher level' 'pre'-figures (not in a temporal so much as an interpretative sense) what takes place on the 'lower' level. That which takes place in heaven or is reported as having its origin in heaven (like the riding forth of the Four Horsemen) offers an insight into a perplexing story of the world. Understanding the mystery of existence is given a new dimension. Events on the earthly stage are enigmatic. One who sees only at the 'lower' level can be offered another perspective on reality by means of the eye of vision. It is that which is the basis of the Apocalypse. It is not that the 'higher' level determines the way in which events below work out. Human beings are not merely puppets at the end of the divine strings. They are confronted with the reality of God and the coming kingdom. That is an inexorable fact which demands understanding and action. So the vision enables the reader to make sense of events and interactions which without that added perspective would seem utterly enigmatic. It is that which can transform understanding, so that what appears to be confusion and folly may be apprehended as the wisdom of God: '... to shame the wise, God has chosen what the world counts folly, and to shame what is strong, God has chosen what the world counts weakness ... The wisdom of this world is folly in God's sight' (I Cor. 1.27; 3.19).

We like our representations of reality to be lifelike and not fantastic. We want to see things 'as they really are'. By that we mean the accuracy of the photograph or video film which captures an event as it happens. It is the television news bulletin which seems to capture the moment of an assassination or the climax of a game which is most prized. It is the news report which tells us exactly 'how it is' which is most to be relied on. However detailed, the prosaic representation of the facts of what confronts us is what we most often take for reality.

But is it so? Can we capture reality merely by looking at something? Is our understanding really so complete by having obtained a representation in word or picture of what happened? The answer of another tradition of interpretation (of which Revelation is a part) is a resounding 'no'. In art, literature, social theory and theology there is a tradition which registers discontent with ways of interpreting our reality which concentrate exclusively on appearances. Appearances are what confront us in the momentary picture. We need analysis, yet analysis is immediately open to human subjectivity and prejudice as dimensions other than what immediately appears are brought into play. In art, pictures to express those dimensions of reality hidden from normal perception yield paintings which may not be true to reality as we think we see it, but in another sense are much more so, because they attempt to 'add on' those other dimensions to a person or situation which are hidden from view but are transparent to the human spirit as it ponders and reflects on what confronts it.

In talking thus we can begin to see a link with apocalyptic. As its name implies, apocalyptic offers an unveiling of that which is hidden and in so doing seeks to lay bare dimensions of existence that are hidden. It does this by speaking of human experience in symbols which have a long history of use. In seeking to present reality in this way we are offered an attempt to paint a fuller picture. Two examples must suffice from Revelation to illustrate the point.

The vision of the Risen Christ in Rev. 1 shows Christ with some unusual features, e.g. the sword proceeding from his mouth. That is a reminder of his role as judge. But he is a judge who is wounded by the brutal treatment of the military. He was himself pierced (Rev. 1.7), a victim of the power of the sword. Likewise his standing in the midst of the lampstands portrays an intimacy of knowledge and relationship which the transcendent thrust of the book may diminish. This intimate relationship is hidden from human gaze and is not to be understood or explained in the language of the 'photographic' representation. The portrayal is in fact more real than a merely prosaic description of those communities could ever be. Similarly the description of the cross which concentrates on the bare chronicle can never adequately represent the reality of what went on. That is graphically portrayed in Rev. 5. This is on a continuum of interpretation with the understanding of the event in the synoptic gospels. In the references to darkness, the rending of the veil etc. (Mark 15.33–38 and parallels), the synoptic gospels have a similar aim. The death of the failed Messiah is seen to be *the* significant moment in human history; for it opens the way to eschatological reality. The full meaning of the bare event is evident to the visionary's eye and expressed in the daring symbolism of the weak, dead Lamb. It is an intuition shared by other New Testament writers. So, for example, the writer of the letter to the Hebrews can expound the death as the moment when heaven and earth were brought together, and the cross of Jesus becomes the moment of his entry behind the heavenly veil (Heb. 6.19f; 9.24).

These intuitions which impel seers and artists to explore hidden dimensions need to be tested but should never be ignored. They may 'see' more than they fully understand in the jumble of images that come together in their work. At other times and in other places others may catch glimpses of that reality they seek to give expression to. Of course, in speaking thus about Revelation there is nothing to separate it from the way in which we interpret any piece of literature. A desire to pin it down to a narrow view of reality both in its original context and in our present situation leads to a cramping of the way in which it can assist our understanding of reality. Provided that we do not continuously demand a close 'photographic' quality, we may find in Revelation the most 'realistic' insight and understanding of our relationships arrangements and the longing of our impoverished world.

What sort of book is Revelation?

This may be a strange kind of question to ask of a book when the opening words seem to make it quite clear that it is an apocalypse (1.1). Yet there are two problems which immediately arise when we take that title seriously.

Firstly, we may ask how John received this revelation? Did he sit down like a poet and exercise that mixture of imagination and attention to form which is characteristic of poetry? Or is the book an account of a visionary experience akin to our dreams? We are never going to be in a position to answer these questions with any confidence. Many commentators suppose that Revelation is a conscious attempt to write an apocalypse much as Paul would have written an epistle. I do not believe that such an assessment is satisfactory. There are many signs in the book itself of that dream-like quality in which the visionary not only sees but is involved (e.g. 1.12; 1.17; 5.4; 7.13; 11.1; 17.3; cf. 1.10 and 21.10). We should pay John the compliment of accepting his claim unless there are strong reasons for denying it. There is a close relationship with the Old Testament, indicating a knowledge which never manifests itself in explicit quotation. Also, there is a semblance of order, which, whatever the reservations of commentators, does yield a coherent pattern and in my view deserves to be made sense of unless the juxtapositions seem totally contradictory. These last mentioned factors suggest that some attempt has been made to give the book shape and coherence, evident in the sayings and exhortations in 1.8ff. and 22.6ff. In this respect Revelation differs markedly from a Jewish apocalypse like I Enoch. By comparison, that is a veritable jumble of heterogeneous material. Such conscious ordering, however, need not exclude the possibility that Revelation contains in whole or in part the visions which John saw. Such visions are familiar to us from the mystical traditions of both Judaism and Christianity. We need not doubt that such experiences were possible at that time.[8]

Secondly, if Revelation is a vision, that does affect the way in which the text is interpreted. The experience of dreams and visions,

---

[8] See C. Rowland, *The Open Heaven: a Study of Apocalyptic in Judaism and Early Christianity*, SPCK 1982.

particularly when, as in the case of Revelation, it contains no interpretation from the visionary, is not susceptible to a definitive quest for the author's intention. The mystery of the visionary mind (whose formation in John's case we can only begin to guess at) makes a certain open-endedness inevitable. Of John's vision it can be said that he wrote so much more than he ever fully understood. Of course, there are some constraints on how we may make sense of it (about which more will be said below). John uses images which are familiar to us from elsewhere and have a fairly well-established meaning. Thus, the contribution of Dan. 7 to the political symbolism of Rev. 13 establishes a frame of reference which will inform (though not determine) the sense we make of that chapter. The importance for us is that the visionary experience, while conditioned by life under Roman dominion, is not determined by it. It is the Beast and Babylon, not Rome and Caesar, which are the vehicles of John's message. As such they have a wider appeal than a narrowly focussed political analysis rooted in particular historical events.

Revelation offers a unique and fascinating possibility for the interpreter in which knowledge of historical context is less important than the sympathy with, and often intuitive insight into, the meaning of the imagery which confronts us in the book. As the history of the interpretation of the book shows, that has met with a bewildering array of possibilities. All we can do is to seek to be true to the text in its totality, to its place in the canon and to ourselves as part of that community which seeks to be faithful to Jesus.

The structure of the Apocalypse

The first three chapters of the book describe the call of John the seer who is imprisoned on the isle of Patmos. That is followed by a series of letters to the angels of the seven churches in Asia Minor in which the heavenly Christ offers reproof and encouragement in varying degrees, encouraging a steadfast witness and the arousal of the complacent from attitudes of compromise. Another dimension of the vision begins in ch. 4 where John sees God enthroned in heaven surrounded by the heavenly host who laud God as Creator and Redeemer. That scene is transformed in the very next chapter which describes the coming of a Lamb to God to receive a sealed scroll. This symbolizes the historical process leading up to the establishment of divine justice on earth. The pattern of three sequences of sevens, most of which concern the disasters which are to befall an unjust and unrepentant world, form a structure which encompasses a large part of chs. 6–19 (where the climax of God's purposes is achieved). Within that scheme we have two passages (chs. 7 and 10–15) which have as their theme the destiny of and the threat to the people of God (the promise of salvation to the persecuted in chs. 7 and 14, the need for a prophetic witness in chs. 10–11, the threat to God's people in chs. 13–13 and the song of deliverance in ch. 15).

An outline of the contents of the book would look something like this:

1.1–8: Introduction
1.9–20: Call vision
2–3: Letters to the seven churches
4: The vision of heaven: a door is opened for the seer to witness the contrast between the acknowledgement of God's sovereignty in the world above and an unresponsive humanity below.
5: The Lamb is shown to be worthy to open the seals and thus to initiate the process of divine judgement and the reconciliation of God and humanity which reaches its climax in 21–22.
6, 8, 9, and 16: The sequence of seals, trumpets and bowls which periodize the eschatological process which must precede the establishment of the divine reign on earth.
7: First interruption in the sequence of seals, trumpets and bowls. The opening of the seals is here interrupted with a description of the sealing of the elect and the promise of ultimate vindication for those who are faithful in the period of divine judgement.
10–15: Second interruption in the sequence – The witness of the church.

10–11: The prophetic task of the church.

12: Divine protection for the people of God and the aknowledgement of ultimate victory but with the imminent threat from the Devil.

13: The earthly embodiment of the Devil in the State revealed and the consequences for those who refuse to compromise.

14: The elect are those who are marked with the mark of the Lamb; they will be the ones to achieve ultimate vindication: the contrast with the fate of those who have the mark of the beast.

15: Song of victory over the enemies of God
17–19.10: Babylon's identity and character revealed and her judgement described.
19.11–21: The victory of the Son of Man over the enemies of God.

20.1–10: The messianic reign on earth with the restraining of evil.
20.11ff.: The last judgement.
21–22.5: New creation, new Jerusalem.
22.6–21: Final admonitions.

This structure suggests the following major themes. First and foremost, the book as a whole offers an account of the resolution of the contrast between heaven and earth, good and evil, in the dwelling of God with men and women in a heaven on earth. The whole of the apocalyptic drama points forward to this. The inexorable unfolding suggests an inevitability about the fulfilment of the divine purposes. There is a determined pattern to the divine purpose whose fulfilment in the last resort does not depend on human consent. The extent of evil and its intractability mean that there is a huge upheaval in order to bring about the establishment of something which is contrary to the will of unrepentant humanity and its perverted institutions. There are hints that there is a divine longing for repentance from humanity (e.g. 9.20) but a grim demonstration of the cost to enable right to prevail. There is a clear perception of the reality of evil and a demonstration of its presence in quarters which might be unexpected, whether in prosperous and well-run churches or the smooth machine of Roman imperial administration. The book stresses the imminence of the fulfilment of some (though not necessarily all) of what is glimpsed by the seer. So the letters emphasize that the present is a moment of opportunity for repentance and vigilance. But there can be no rushing the divine purposes. In this situation patience and endurance are important virtues. The vision of what is to come offers a means of carrying on in inauspicious circumstances, whether there be a threat to discipleship from persecution or from complacency.

How our Christian brothers and sisters have interpreted the text

The suspicion which Revelation attracts in many of the mainstream churches contrasts with its central role in the theology of many Christians in previous generations. Isaac Newton and William Blake are two examples. It has empowered change and has been a happy hunting ground for speculation about the end of the world. Martin Luther had a low opinion of the book of Revelation because it did not preach Christ, and his assessment probably typifies the responses of many to the enigmas of the book:

About this book of the Revelation of John, I leave everyone free to hold his own ideas, and would bind no man to my opinion and judgement: I say what I feel. I miss more than one thing in this book, and this makes me hold it to be neither apostolic or prophetic. First and foremost, the Apostles do not deal with visions, but prophesy in clear, plain words, as do Peter and Paul and Christ in the gospel. For it befits the apostolic office to speak of Christ and his deeds without figures and visions; but there is no prophet in the Old Testament, to say nothing of the New, who deals so out and out with visions and figures. And so I think of it almost as I do of the Fourth Book of Esdras, and I can in nothing detect that it was provided by the Holy Spirit.

Moreover, he seems to be going much too far when he commends his own book so highly, – more than any other of the sacred books do, though they are much more important, and threaten that if any one takes away anything from it, God will deal likewise with him. Again, they are to be blessed who keep what is written therein; and yet no one knows what that is, to say nothing of keeping it. It is just the same as if we had not, and there are many far better books for us to keep. Many of the fathers rejected, too, this book of old, though St Jerome, to be sure, praises it highly and says that it is above all praise and that there are as many mysteries in it as words; though he cannot prove this at all, and his praise is at many points too mild.

Finally, let every one think of it as his own spirit gives him to think. My spirit cannot fit itself into this book. There is one sufficient reason for me not to think highly of it – Christ is not taught or known in it; but to teach Christ is the thing which an apostle above all else is bound to do, as He says in Acts 1 'Ye shall be my witnesses'. Therefore I stick to the books which give me Christ clearly and purely.[9]

As a way of marking his distaste for Revelation, Luther consigned the book (along with Hebrews, James and Jude) to the very end of the New Testament, thus drawing attention to what he perceived as the theological shortcomings and dangers to be found in the book. For him, clearly, it was little better than a book in the apocrypha. Two

[9] Martin Luther, *Preface to the New Testament*, quoted from W. G. Kümmel, *The New Testament: the History of the Investigation of its Problems*, ET Abingdon and SCM Press 1972, pp. 25f.

major shortcomings are cited: not teaching Christ and the absence of plain words to express the gospel. So many of *our* suspicions about Revelation suggest that we echo that view and should not be surprised that such a distinguished Christian teacher should have expressed such a negative view. All of us want simple expressions of truth. The assumption that this is what we have elsewhere in the New Testament in contrast with Revelation is hardly borne out by the enigmatic character of the parables. Jesus stresses their puzzling character (hence we find the disciples frequently needing further elucidation – Matt. 13.35). That is all very different from the familiar homely tales of popular imagination!

We shall not be surprised to hear that there were doubts expressed in the early church about the canonical status of the book (some thought that it was the product of an early Christian heretic, called Cerinthus). Such negative opinions need to be balanced by the views of those who have found in it a clue to the meaning of history. Hippolytus, a Roman bishop at the beginning of the third century AD, found in the imagery of the Antichrist (not a term found in Revelation) in Rev. 13 a potent symbol of his age, drawing as it did on the tradition stemming from Daniel of the empires of the world being symbolized by beasts. Augustine interpreted the account of the messianic reign of Christ in Revelation 20 as a description of the era of the church, thus evacuating the passage of its message of hope for the future of this world. In the middle ages the Italian monk Joachim of Fiore wrote complicated commentaries on Revelation and saw in its imagery predictions of the imminent flowering of spiritual life as a herald to the reign of God on earth.

It has not just been our ancestors in the faith who have resorted to Revelation, however. In our day Christians who are at opposite ends of the political spectrum have found in its images a resource of hope and a description of the climax of human history. The point is made in the following comments about religion in the contemporary USA:

> The book of Revelation has been many things to many men [sic]. Above all, it has been a poem of hope to oppressed Christians throughout the ages, an empowering poem. In our day, Daniel Berrigan, for example, finds inspiration in Revelation for his antinuclear activism. Writing in 1976 from a District of Columbia jail, Berrigan reflects on the experience of John, the author of Revelation, in exile on the island of Patmos, and concludes that prisons are a 'natural seedbed of visionaries'.

... (Also) in our own day, the book of Revelation more often serves as a dream of miraculous rescue and as a license for escape from struggle. The panoramas of destruction, depicted in loving detail, with no human solution offered but the flight from the world, are helping to create the conditions through which they become scenes from a self-fulfilling prophecy.[10]

Thus does A. Mojtabai describe the way in which New Testament passages, in particular those concerned with the rapture of the elect before the earth is finally engulfed by catastrophe, undergird the thinking of many Christians who live and work in the shadow of a nuclear weapon factory in Texas.

In the USA the book of Revelation forms a significant part of a reading of biblical prophecy, popularized by Hal Lindsey in his book *The Late Great Planet Earth*.[11] In this a complicated dramatic scenario is expounded leading to the salvation of the elect and the degeneration of human history into a nuclear holocaust. Outside the mainstream Christian churches the Jehovah's Witnesses have looked to the book of Revelation for their simple account of the climax of human history. Their political quietism is a salutary reminder that the book is not solely the preserve of political and religious radicals. What distinguishes these two types of interpretation is the treatment of the imagery and the application of the contents of the book to *present* political realities and Christian responses to them.

In the Hal Lindsey reading of Revelation the visions are woven into a tapestry of biblical prophecy which relates more or less literally to future happenings which accompany the end of the world. From a very different political perspective the South African theologian, Allan Boesak, finds in Revelation a message of comfort and a resource for protest in the struggle against the apartheid regime in South Africa. He treats the visions as having contemporary relevance, the full understanding of which demands attention to the social and political world of the text as well as that of the interpreter:

John writes about the political situation in Asia Minor in his day and of the response of the church to that situation; his book cannot be understood outside of the political context of his time. But it is also prophecy. However, no prophecy receives its full and final

---

[10] A.G. Mojtabai, *Blessed Assurance: at Home with the Bomb in Amarillo, Texas*, Secker and Warburg 1987, p. 163.
[11] Hal Lindsey, *The Late Great Planet Earth*, Zondervan 1970, Bantam Books 1974.

fulfilment in one given historical moment only, or even in a series of events. If the prophecy is the expression of an undeniable truth which comes from God, it will be fulfilled at different times and in different ways in the history of the world ... *What was true in the time of John is proven to be true over and over again in the history of the church of Jesus Christ in the world* (my italics) ... this is why Revelation is so relevant for us today ... because we see with some astonishment how truly, how authentically, that John, in describing his own time, is describing the time in which we live. Apocalypse for John thus meant God's final judgment on the corrupt and religious systems of oppression.[12]

Bearing such matters in mind will equip us for the quest for a critical reflection on the scriptures and our use of them in order to be better able to lay bare the role they are playing in ideological struggles in different social contexts. We need a critical awareness of the choices we make in interpreting a book like Revelation.

A prime task of the exegete is to watch the way in which the biblical material is being and has been *used*. In so doing it is necessary to make sure that readers are engaged with the text in its various parts and are as attentive as possible to it. There is more than meets the eye in the way in which we are wont to read and use the scriptures. That may well be because our churches school us to read in particular ways because of the ways in which particular texts are juxtaposed.

It is necessary to contribute alternative horizons to our contemporary use of scripture. Firstly, we may do this by exploring to the full what might have been the original setting and cirumstances of the various texts *as well as the history of interpretation within and outside the Bible* as a challenge to the belief that our application of the texts tells the whole story of their meaning. Secondly, the language of the reign of God itself offers an alternative perspective on the arrangements of the present. A broader horizon is offered and the reader is asked to consider the present in the light of the threat of judgement and the glory of the age to come. There is a protest against those arrangements which have the appearance of order but which in reality have brought about the prosperity and progress of some at the expense of others. It is frequently those who have to bear that suffering who can see the fragility of those structures which appear to offer peace and security. Those whose lives are broken and who

---

[12] Allan Boesak, *Comfort and Protest*, St Andrew Press 1987, pp. 28f.

live at the margins can discern the signs of the times in ways which are frightening to those of us who cannot see from what is apparently a more favoured vantage-point. Many throughout history have been attentive in ways which would not be possible for those in more comfortable surroundings, for whom life does not seem to present such stark choices or an oppressive threat. It is incumbent upon us to attend to them, and the book of Revelation encourages us to think that the suffering Christ may be in their midst, siding with them and reproaching the more prosperous of us.

Reading Revelation

There are several ways of interpreting Revelation. We can treat it as a relatively straightforward account of the end of the world, in which all the details contained in it relate not to present ecclesiastical and political realities but that which is still to come in the future, however imminent. Secondly, we can ignore the contemporary impact of the visions by taking an entirely historical perspective and seeking only to place the visions in the (ancient) context. In such an interpretation questions are concerned with the meaning for the original author and readers. Thirdly, there can be a form of interpretation which refuses to see the welter of images as a straightforward description of the end of the world but relates them primarily to the inward journey of the soul to God. Fourthly, there is another form of present application which sees the images as having a limited (though not exclusive) application to the present situation of the church in the world, even if there was a particular relevance, still partially recoverable, for the churches in Asia Minor in the first century AD.

It is this fourth tradition of interpretation (akin to that espoused by Boesak earlier) which will be espoused in this commentary. The choice of it depends on the assumption that the symbolism is not exhausted by any one set of social and political circumstances, nor is its powerful message so obviously confined to future events as to make use of it as a comment on our present affairs illegitimate. Indeed, as will become apparent in the commentary the visions are not exclusively concerned with the end of the world. Thus, the vision of the vindication of the Lamb in Rev. 5, the identity of the true prophet in ch. 11 and the nature of the abuse of power in chs. 13 and 17 illuminate issues in John's day and our own.

A contemporary concern can open the door to outrageous and

unchecked contemporary applications of its imagery. That is not something that is without precedent in church history, of course. The identification of the whore of Babylon with the Pope or the Beast from the Land as the World Council of Churches in more recent writing will remind us of that. It does not seem to me that a remedy against this kind of identification is the total avoidance of an interpretation whose concern is primarily contemporary. Fear of getting it wrong has led interpreters to be reluctant to offer suggestions about the way Revelation's symbols can offer insights on the character of contemporary institutions. Such a reluctance smacks too much of an over-reaction against outrageous identification.

If we look at the way in which the book of Revelation has been interpreted down the centuries, we shall find its imagery being used to elucidate responses to a variety of situations in which Christians find themselves confronted by terrible evil and oppressive social systems. Doubtless some thought that the visions applied solely to their own day: *they* were the ones to whom alone John's visions were speaking. There is something similar in the ways in which we find Revelation used today. Minute analysis can convince readers that the meaning of the symbols relates precisely to the historical circumstances of *their* day. Revelation becomes a book of exclusive relevance to ourselves and *our* generation alone. It is that exclusiveness I want to challenge in this commentary. My reading is of a more general kind but one that seeks to relate the symbols of Revelation to the struggle for God's justice in every generation. I cannot prove that this is the most obvious way of reading Revelation, nor can I with certainty refute those who would find detailed prescriptions of contemporary history in Revelation's symbolism. I lack the confidence to be so certain about that. Yet I am convinced in Revelation that we have a book which should not, in effect, be ignored until we can be sure that the end of the age is upon us. I believe that it still speaks to those who live in the midst of the old order, looking for something better but unconvinced that ours is the last generation before the Kingdom of God comes in all its fullness.

Dealing with apocalyptic symbols

Revelation presents particular problems for the interpreter. We seem to be confronted with a foreign language which we do not understand. It provokes that mixture of incomprehension and distaste. Almost from the very start (and certainly when we get to ch.4 with its beasts and other bizarre imagery) we find ourselves in an alien world, more akin to the fantasy world of science fiction than religion. That recognition, however, is important. Revelation does not offer a view of things in any kind of literal way. Reading Revelation is much like reading a good and pungent political cartoon. It will infuriate and offend and yet also pierce to the heart of the pretence of our political processes in a way which the well-argued piece of prose often cannot. It is fantastic, imaginative and strange. Like all exercises in imagination it demands of us that we are prepared to suspend our down to earth reservations and to enter into its world. We may have to exercise our imaginations and look at things in a different way. That may be no bad thing when our outlook is governed so often by a rationality which can justify the inhumane and barbaric.

But what more barbaric book is there than the book of Revelation, with its catalogue of disasaster and destruction apparently sanctioned by God (e.g. chs. 6 and 8)? Can we take seriously a book which seems so contrary to the spirit of Jesus? In reacting in this way we may be tempted, as so many Christians have been down the centuries, to consign it to the margins of our concern and leave it to the religious fanatics and others who seem to find some comfort in it. But is the matter as simple as that? Can we with integrity ignore so easily a book which is central to the canon just because we cannot cope very well with its outlook? Instead of posing Revelation as the problem, perhaps we ought to ask ourselves why we have so much difficulty with the book? Is it asking awkward questions of ourselves and our view of the world which we would prefer not to face up to? Is it posing questions about our understanding of the Christian gospel which we might prefer to ignore, because of the amount of rethinking it would involve us in about the meaning of Christianity? Such issues are particularly pressing when we remember that the book of Revelation is a constant inspiration for millions of Christians in the Third World who find in it a way of looking at the world which challenges its present arrangements and offers hope of something different based on God's justice.

We prefer things that are down to earth and normal. We like people to call a spade a spade and to be practical rather than airy-fairy about things. We like 'realistic' writing better than poetry because it seems to be more real. But therein lies the problem. What we perceive as real may be far from being the whole story (indeed, it may even offer us a distorted version of it). Artists and poets have

33

long recognized that writing prose can never do justice to the full dimension of human experience. So they have resorted either to forms of words or images which seek to offer a different dimension on what we perceive to be real. Through their words or their eyes we can suddenly be aware of dimensions to life that we had been blind or deaf to. That is something of which we are particularly in need. Supposedly sophisticated minds are often so impoverished; our vision is narrow, and the exercise of our imagination so feeble. So when we read visions such as we have in the book of Revelation, we get bogged down in questions about whether things would literally turn out like this.

We have got so used to supposing that what words refer to must correspond directly with what we read in the text. Jesus spoke of minds so little attuned to the divine wisdom when he gave thanks that God had revealed true wisdom to 'babes' (Matt. 11.25f.). When Christ appears amidst the seven-branched candlestick we are bemused by the pictures and tempted to read it as if we were reading an actual description of something that existed in the world. No, we must read Revelation differently. We must read it as if we were reading poetry or looking at a painting. That means being prepared to see things from another, unusual, point of view and being open to the possibility that difference of perspective will enrich our view and lead to difference of insight. Surely, that is only appropriate when we come to talk about the climax of history where photographic precision was never intended and a literalistic interpretation of the images would reduce their power? When we think of Christ coming on the clouds of heaven, we may want to visualize it, but, in so doing, we shall reduce the power of the symbol. That refers to something real, but what precisely it refers to cannot be spelt out with certainty. We have to remain content with the symbols of power and glory and vindication. Yet words alone cannot begin to convey with any sense of completeness the nature of our hope.

Freud was not the first to attach significance to dreams, though his systematic description of them on the basis of a scientific psychology was novel. In all cultures dreams speak of another way of looking at things; they are a door on to another reality. In our dreams bits of our experience surface in our minds in strange and, sometimes frightening, ways. Dreams represent parts of ourselves that we would usually like to keep hidden from our conscious selves. They are messages, often difficult to decipher, which we give to ourselves about parts of our life which may need attention or which have been neglected.[13] We shall always need to approach dreams with care, for claims to comprehension are often fraught with self-deception. They will defy our attempts to reduce them to tidy explanations. Mostly, we forget our dreams unless there was something particularly bizarre or frightening about them. We will not always make sense of them, even if we can get the drift of the story they are telling. But often they may show up attitudes and feelings which we would prefer not to recognize.

Dreaming is an important part of our lives. It has a therapeutic effect but in particular can bring to our awareness, if we have eyes to see, dimensions of living which can so easily become buried by everyday patterns of thinking which characterize our waking lives. It is no wonder that in the ancient world (and today in non-western cultures) dreams are regarded with such importance. In the Bible it is Joseph's capacity to dream and to interpret the dreams that gives him so much wisdom and power (Gen. 40.5ff.). The same is true for Daniel. Of course, dreamers and the interpreters of dreams are not always to be trusted (Deut. 13). Nevertheless they have a potent role to play in making people aware of the hidden dimension to existence, and revealing truths which might otherwise be concealed (something which is very apparent in the role played by dreams in the infancy narratives in Matthew's gospel).

The world of dreams is akin to that less ordered imaginative part of ourselves. Just as we attend too little to dreams, so we lack the developed skills which enable us to exercise our imaginations. Our quest for order resists flights of fancy. We prefer the prosaic and the ordinary. Our imaginations are out of condition. That means that we are in no fit state to read Revelation with real sympathy.

A way of appreciating a little more the character of the visions in Revelation and the way in which to approach their interpretation is to explore further the comparison of the verbal images there with the visual images in some contemporary art. This book includes some examples of prints by Kip Gresham on the themes of Revelation. We may immediately react by terming them very abstract. That is, they do not immediately correspond to our everyday experience. We might go on and say that our preference is for something more true to life . But let us instead attempt to stay with the pictures and ask what they mean *for us*. That may take some doing. It may be rather like taking exercise and finding ourselves 'out of condition' and using

[13] See Charles Rycroft, *The Innocence of Dreams*, Hogarth Press, 1979, reissued 1992.

muscles which are weak and under-used. Similarly, the exercise of our imagination will leave us emotionally breathless and out of condition. We are not used to doing it. We may want to take a short cut by asking what it was that the author intended by the work of art. That is an interesting question. Let us be clear that this does not solve the interpretative problem for us. We still have to make sense of that text for ourselves. Ultimately, what is most important is what emotions images, words and sounds elicit from us. We must learn to use and even create for ourselves interpretative skills in areas of our response which may be rather underdeveloped as compared with our facility to explain and rationalize. In this respect the poverty of our imagination differs from those who may be less literate than we are. For them pictures, cartoons, and the verbal pictures of Revelation with all its drama may be immediately appealing and more able to communicate to them than to us.

But back to our pictures. Look at each one in turn. Note your immediate reactions, however outlandish they may be. When you have done that, ask yourself why it was that you reacted in the way in which you did. That pattern applies in exactly the same way to reading the biblical text, particularly a text like the book of Revelation. With Kip Gresham's pictures we could, if we were so minded, compare our interpretations with his. We cannot do that with the author of the book of Revelation. We can conjecture what the symbolism might have meant to him and to his reader; but that is all. For that reason especially we must have the courage to exercise our imagination and ask what the text means for us.

But what happens when we have rival interpretations of the same vision? That is an issue which applies right across the field of biblical interpretation and has attended discussions of scripture throughout the history of the church. The issue here, however, is not whether there is a right or wrong interpretation leaping out of the text at us demanding that we apprehend it. Rather it concerns the ways in which power struggles among the interpreters themselves and the traditions they represent are brought to a conclusion. Some interpretations are obviously excluded. It is a Lamb slain and not a cat or a dog that is exalted to God's throne. The context of interpretation is the language and imagery of the Bible which may assist, though not determine, our understanding. It is a vindication of the way of Christ, not some other, which is offered. When it comes to the meaning of visions and particular symbols, we shall have to recognize the refusal of apocalyptic symbolism to be tied down to one particular meaning. While images do not mean *anything* that we care to want them to mean, there are very few indications that the text 'demands' that we use as a key to the interpretation of the whole. As a reader I am in the position of resorting to a variety of means to make sense of the text. I might resort to finding parallels with passages in the Old Testament or contemporary Jewish and Christian literature. But these other texts cannot be determinative for the way in which I read. I have to remember that Revelation itself is a product of a *visionary* mind saturated in apocalyptic symbols which are the product of a fertile imagination, so the earlier context and use cannot always determine the way in which I interpret the passage.

We need also to remember that Revelation was a product of a particular time and place. John too was part of a social and economic world which inhibited and provoked him. He was not part of the powerful élite who ran the world for their advantage. Indeed, he above all New Testament writers produced a book which is most sensitive to the injustice of the powerful. We always need to remember that just as our reading of texts like Revelation reflect our own concerns and prejudices, so also the writers of the biblical books exhibit their own concerns and limitations within the political and economic world of their day.[14]

Constrained by Christ: Can we read Revelation in any way we like?

From what I have written so far it might appear that the history of interpretation of this text leaves unanswered the quesion: can I read this text in whatever way I like? Of course, there is nothing to stop us doing that. But if we read as Christians we do so within the constraints of the community of faith. There is a responsibility and a discipline. We need to be able to command a hearing for our way of looking at the text in that other readers are going to be in a position of saying 'Yes, that makes sense to me.' That is part of what it means to read the text as part of a community. We can be as extravagant and as idiosyncratic as we like in the way we interpret. What we cannot demand is that we have the right to insist that our reading has to be adopted by everyone else and, in particular, that it counts as a reading of the text which counts as part of the Christian community's story.

[14] See Itumeleng Mosala, *Biblical Hermeneutics and Black Theology in South Africa*, Eerdmans 1989.

Confronting the powers and the demons in others and in the institutions of church and state must be accompanied by the task of confronting them and overcoming them in ourselves. Individual champions of sacred causes who feel the need to leave behind the critical support of the people of God are particularly vulnerable to self-deception. All too easily the human ego can demand satisfaction of its needs in the promotion of a good cause with the result that the cause itself can become subordinated to that need. But to be honest about ourselves does not diminish the importance of the task of the church to confront the powers in conformity with the ministry of Jesus. The account of that struggle with evil in the story of Jesus which portrays the internal temptation continuing throughout the ministry (e.g. Temptation, Peter's Confession and immediate identification with Satan in Mark 8.30 and 8.33) is a reminder of the careful process which is involved in recognizing communally (particularly within the church) the demonic at work even in all those institutions and motives which claim to be part of the new aeon.

If I were to expound Revelation in such a way that I found in its images an incitement to armed insurrection to establish a new heaven and earth, there would be widespread protest. That reaction would arise for a variety of reasons. Some would arise from an inbuilt conservatism in the Christian community; others because of a deep unease about compatibility with the gospel. It is the latter that is of particular concern. First of all, not only has Revelation not been read in that way by the majority of Christians but also there has been a steadfast refusal to see the ongoing story of Christianity being exemplified by resort to arms. However bad the Christian church has been at keeping to that vision in practice, it has been unable to shake off the fact that the fundamental story which shapes its life is of a crucified Messiah who refused armed struggle as a way of inaugurating the kingdom of God (Matt. 26.53; John 18.36). Secondly, we would look at the text itself and in the midst of what appears to be an orgy of destruction we *never* find the people of God being called on to assist in a process of destruction and disintegration.

There is never going to be any faultless guide to interpretation. At present we see in a glass darkly and not with the perfection still to come. Indeed, we must not expect our interpretative map to be full of the authoritative detail which would guarantee a correct route. Reading a map, however detailed, depends on the interpreter for its correct use. That will involve correct appreciation of the symbols involved, the orientation of the map and the 'external' factor of the direction and perspective of the user. It is so easy to misread a map and go off in the wrong direction!

Such points are apposite to any consideration of how we use scripture. Unlike the map we are not supplied with a key to the symbols used in Revelation. Yet a Christian reading of it has a key in the person of Christ, though the content of that in practice remains to be decided in each situation. What characterizes Paul's commitment, for example, is conformity to Christ (I Cor. 11.1). The outworking of that depends on the indwelling Spirit as well as engagement with the tradition within the circumstances in which he found himself. The same is true of us. For us the tradition is embodied particularly in the fourfold story of Jesus' career. The Christian creeds stress that in the life of Jesus our understanding of God is to be understood, so we are driven back to the scriptural witness to the life of Jesus, in its nuanced diversity. If we seek to find some bearings in our use of Revelation, we shall find ourselves bound to orient them on his faithful witness (3.14). This is precisely what Revelation demands. At the heart of the vision in ch. 5 is the Lamb who was slain. He has the key to past, present and future (1.18; 22.13). He it is who is ruler of the nations (12.5; 19.16). Throughout its apocalyptic imagery the book of Revelation radiates an exalted Christology which helped form the basis for Trinitarian theology.

In refusing to allow the readers to rest complacent with their lot Revelation coincides with the major thrust of the final eschatological discourse of Jesus (Matt. 24–25; Mark 13; Luke 21). What it promised the disciple is ultimate vindication (though the gospels dwell on this only briefly). Throughout there is a sombre tone of warning, the need for alertness and readiness to bear witness in the midst of a world which is increasingly disordered. Dreams of a new society and complacency about the present are not alluded to. The tone of the eschatological discourses is stark and devoid of warmth and ease. It is not surprising that many have thought that these chapters are products of the early church. It is tempting to wrest Jesus away from these dark prognostications and preserve him for our comfort and assurance. But these chapters form an integral part of the portrait of Jesus, and are an understandable component of the dark hours before Jesus' arrest and execution. In the gloomy circumstances of the rejection of the message in Jerusalem and the imminent betrayal by one of the inner circle, a note of foreboding and the greater intensity of judgement is entirely understandable. The optimism of the proclamation of the kingdom of God and the acclamation of the

Galilean crowds dissipates in the face of the encircling gloom of death.

It is that tone which pervades Revelation, though it too does not lack the optimism of Jesus' Galilean ministry. As such it continues the atmosphere appropriate for the period between the advents of the Messiah. The totality of the witness of Jesus in life and death undergirds Revelation and must undergird interpretations of it. Any interpretation which ends up in naive complacency or self-congratulatory celebration is as deluded as one that is guilty of 'baptizing' the *status quo* and ignores the element of judgement which pervades the story of Jesus. Our interpretations must not be without hope but must be rooted in specific practice and suspicion of the precise constructions of reality that confront us. The hope of God in Christ challenges our self-satisfaction and preoccupation with things as they are. It consistently challenges readers to see the inadequacies and impoverishment of present arrangements.

The claim to prophetic insight is one that is fraught with problems. The divine wisdom may enlighten, but there are occasions when such claims can be diabolically destructive. Throughout the Bible prophecy is a central component of life, and yet is also highly problematic. The very nature of prophecy means that it is not subject to control by sets of regulations. What happens when there are contrasting presentations of the word of God? John's apocalyptic prophecy obviously did not stand alone (and possibly not unchallenged) in the churches of his day. This is an issue which confronts us in Revelation where John condemns 'Jezebel' and the pseudo-prophetic witness of the Beast and its agent (Rev. 13; cf. 19.20). In the Old Testament the issue attracted attention (Jer. 19; Deut. 13 and 18). According to Revelation a claim to speak for God which involved accommodation with the existing order (2.20) is to be repudiated. Similarly in Deut. 13 it is the prophetic exhortation to worship other gods and be like the other nations which is the mark of false prophecy.

Nowhere is the difficulty of testing the prophetic spirit more acute than in Jeremiah's time (Jer. 23.9; 27.9). He is confronted with prophets who proclaim peace and security, probably appealing to deeply ingrained religious sentiments about the inviolability of Zion, God's holy dwelling place. In Jeremiah's case we find the prophet groping towards a view of prophetic ministry which found a clear articulation in Jesus' view that the true prophet can expect to suffer for his message (Luke 11.49). Jeremiah's experience of persecution and rejection led to some of the most remarkable outbursts of the prophetic tradition, linking the experience of obedience to its negative social and psychological consequences. That link between message and life becomes a test of true prophecy in the early Christian writing, e.g. Matt. 7.15; and in the Didache 11–13 (an early Christian manual of church life and morals), where itinerant prophets have been causing problems for the small Christian communities. The solution is based on life-style: the satisfaction of self-interest is regarded as evidence of false prophecy. The prophet can expect to suffer because s/he will have to utter unpalatable things, yet care needs to be taken to avoid undue rigidity, so that unnecessary provocation, paranoia and masochism become the mark of the prophet. Also it is important to remember that even Balaam, who is reviled as a false teacher (Rev. 2.15; II Peter 2.15; Jude 11) and is remembered as one who led Israel astray (Num. 31.10) can on occasion utter true prophetic words (Num. 24.16)!

Finally, the form of the book of Revelation offers us clues to our interpretation. The letters to the churches keep us down to earth. They turn our gaze to the ordinary things and make us see their momentous significance from the point of view of God's reign of justice and peace. John's summons to prophesy in ch. 10 reinforces the fact that this is not simply a mind-blowing apocalyptic drama in the face of which we merely watch with stupefied gaze. Indeed, things like buying and selling and the 'ordinary' forms of social behaviour such as reverence for the State and the imperial power can have eternal consequences. It is as if Jesus' words in the Sermon on the Mount ('You cannot serve God and Mammon') are commented on in the apocalyptic symbolism. Revelation seems to suggest that there is nothing neutral in life. Every part of human existence in its use can be a force for good or evil. The value of the insignificant and forgettable is shown up for the enormity of its import for good or ill.

The Old Testament provides the mode of discourse of the book and yet it is never formally quoted. It indicates the vitality of the Jewish religious tradition. Babylon, Sodom, Balaam, Jezebel, Paradise, the Beast with horns and eyes and the living creatures are not merely images of a dead tradition which is part of a nation's history. They are the living means of speaking about persons and events and giving meaning to human existence. This is not the language and mythology of the dominant culture of the day but of a relatively obscure, despised sect of a people who kept themselves aloof from the mainstream of culture.

The idiosyncratic and (by the standards of the day) barbaric Greek syntax also deserves to be mentioned. It will not be apparent to us when we read the English translation, but the Greek of Revelation is full of 'bad' grammar. It is rather like Dialect English or pidgin English as compared with 'Queen's' or 'BBC' English. It may well have been the case that it was written by a person who did not know the rules of Greek grammar well and thought and wrote naturally in Hebrew or Aramaic. Whatever the reason, the grammar's non-conformity is a telling reminder that its message as a whole refuses to conform to what is normal or commonsense. John writes as an exile, an outsider, an insignificant person in the face of the might of Rome. Yet he is the one who is privileged to glimpse the mystery of God's purposes. The very strangeness of the imagery pulls us up short. We may well immediately react with distaste or bewilderment and look elsewhere. Instead of turning aside, let us examine that negative reaction. Could it be the case that this strange, often repulsive, imagery is telling us, perhaps even reminding us of something unpalatable about ourselves, our world, even our religion which we would prefer not to face up to? Is the strangeness of this book rubbing our noses in the fact that God's ways are not our ways and God's thoughts not our thoughts (Isa. 40ff.)?

Revelation and certainty

The appeal to revelation can offer an easy answer to intractable human problems through divinely bestowed insight. It can in some circumstances be an antidote to a radical pessimism which despairs of ever being able to make sense of the contradictions of human existence. The only way forward in such circumstances can appear to be complete reliance on the revelation of God to a fallible and inadequate humanity unable to understand or act from its own resources. In general terms we may suppose that something of this was at work in the apocalyptic culture which flourished at the time of Revelation. It could breed a mood of acute despair and depreciation of human ability to make sense of history. That in turn led to a rejection of all but the revealed word or vision which answers all the problems of existence. Yet despite their claims to divine revelation apocalypses do not offer unambiguous and exclusive answers. They can produce as much mystification as enlightenment. Some visions themselves do not always offer an unambiguous answer to questions. Indeed, there is frequently need for interpretation of enigmatic dreams and visions sometimes provided by an accompanying angel (Rev. 7.13; 17.7). The story of the interpretation of Revelation offers evidence of the perplexity caused by a work which purports to reveal and yet so often ends up leaving us confused and bewildered.

Some apocalypses refuse to provide 'answers' through revelation and offer nothing more than the assertion that understanding is beyond the human mind to grasp. Instead there is an the emphasis on the present struggle. This is especially apparent in IV Ezra (also known as II Esdras, which is in the Apocrypha). Here issues of theodicy are particular apparent. The seer wishes to know why Israel has been allowed to suffer and why God seems content to allow the bulk of humanity to perish. There is stress on the puny nature of human understanding in the face of the transcendence of God, on the ultimate victory of God's righteousness and on the need for those committed to the ways of God to continue in that way in order to achieve eternal life. Dreams of the future are subordinated to the present obedience in the face of human injustice. Here there is no solution but struggle. No dramatic interventions of God are allowed through enlightenment or angelic battles to rescue the righteous from the present struggle.

Christian experience has always oscillated between claims to absolute truth and certainty on the one hand and doubt verging at times on despair on the other. At one time or another we have all been tempted to unravel the knot we find ourselves tied in by resort to authoritative claims to have found the clue to existence. In all of us there is a deep desire to *know*, as the early Christian gnostics put it, 'whence we have come and whither we are going'. People with a simple, clear and authoritative message can appeal to and attract huge followings because they offer clarity of vision and purpose and can get things done. Those of us who muddle through because our perception of God and the world prevents us from seeing things in such clear-cut terms can by contrast seem to be vaccillating and uncertain.

Apocalyptic may seem to pander to the desire for certainty and the unambiguous divine directive. Here after all is the voice from beyond which bursts like a flash of lightning into the greyness of our world and shows things up in their true colours. Temporizing and uncertainty seem out of the question in the face of the crisis provoked by this irruption of clarity. There is some truth in that assessment of apocalyptic and there is much that is written in this commentary which explores the importance of the unmasking of reality as an essential ingredient in the task of exploring God's will. What Revelation primarily does is to refuse to allow the ambiguities of existence to be the basis for inaction.

What is dangerous is that dimension of apocalyptic which lays claim to revelation and brooks no dispute. Here one perspective is deemed to be right and all else hopelessly misguided. That kind of perspective is endemic to religion. This is particularly true of the three great Abrahamic religions: Judaism, Christianity and Islam. At the centre of all of them are claims to revelation: the Torah, the Bible, the Quran, Jesus Christ. Appeals to fundamentals want to get back to the essence of the revelation as the basis of true religion. Judaism has sanctified the process of interpretation and raised to authoritative status the ongoing practice of revelation (as in practice has Islam). Christianity also demands that the interpretation of the Torah must be viewed through the story of the life and death of Christ and the same Spirit which still informs the lives of the followers of the Messiah.

Whatever may be the case in other religions, therefore, Christianity cannot be viewed as a religion of revelation of unambiguous verities. Despite the claims to the contrary, the words of the Bible do not offer a consistent pattern of behaviour and clear-cut moral pattern. Those who seem to know the 'Christian' view on this or that subject are frequently selective in their choice of passage. Biblical morality often turns out to be much less clear-cut than it is often claimed to be. Even faithfulness to the person of Christ has elicited a range of responses. Our experience over two thousand years may have narrowed the range of options somewhat, but that does not prevent us from unwillingness to expect obedience *au pied de la lettre* to all Jesus' words (something Paul was himself unwilling to do, according to I Cor. 9.14).

Despite the authoritative status it claims for itself the book of Revelation hardly claims to offer the last word on any subject. It offers clear-cut convictions on the centrality of Christ, the importance of a distinctive Christian life-style, of prophetic witness and intense suspicion of the values of the surrounding culture and institutions. It nowhere lays down precise rules of how these issues should be responded to. For example, how one decides what is food sacrificed to idols (there is much less discussion than in I Cor. 8), how one distinguishes true and false apostles, what is wrong with the teaching of the Nicolaitans and what is involved in compromise with the State are left unspecified. Its christological concern points us to the story of Jesus (though nothing is said in Revelation about the details of his life). Its symbolism excludes certainty. At first sight we may think that here at last we have *the* authoritative pronouncement. But we deceive ourselves if we think that the pronouncement leaves us (and equally important, the Spirit) superfluous to the process of understanding. We are not offered a code of law which is detailed and immediately applicable but a mystery which seems to cover up at the very moment it appears to reveal. There is no authoritative interpreter to tell us exactly what it means (a significant difference as compared, say, with Daniel 2 and 7ff.). We are not left in darkness but nor are we in the clear light of the detailed, unambiguous knowledge for which we crave. We are not treated like children who need to have everything explained. The apocalypse shocks our sensibilities and can heighten our awareness; it does not offer us a precise recipe for life or faith. The manifestation of God's wrath is in part meant to open our eyes to the distortion of the present and lead us to repent as a result (9.20). But it is possible that what is revealed may end up hardening our hearts (cf. Mark 4.11f.). If we do have eyes to see and ears to hear, that new perspective offered by the apocalypse can help us make a start on exploring how we may live differently and honour the Creator in our deeds as well as our words.

Light and darkness: the importance of Revelation's view of the world

One of the most striking features of Revelation is the way it seeks to differentiate sharply between good and evil. Theologically, socially and psychologically these are key matters. There are those who seek to keep themselves pure and unspotted from the world and those who argue that some kind of accommodation with the old order is inevitable, and indeed necessary.[15] If adherents of a religion have a clear set of goals and a self-awareness which is militantly 'alternative' to the prevailing culture, there is always going to be a desire on their part to ensure the purity of the message is preserved from contamination. That may mean a conscious separation of the group from the wider world, whether by physical separation or psychological distance. There are degrees of intensity of this process. With regard to the communal separation, various forms of monasticism involve varying degrees of separation from the wider society in order to

[15] See the classic discussion in H.R. Niebuhr, *Christ and Culture*, Faber & Faber 1952.

maintain a distinctive style of life. There are those who, while living as part of the ordinary society, separate themselves mentally in their behaviour. In Christianity there have always been those who have wanted to argue for the compatibility, indeed superiority, of Christianity and would stress the importance of arguing for Christianity's reasonableness in terms familiar to the wider society. Continuity between church and society is the order of the day. On the other hand (and the book of Revelation falls in this category) there have been those who have maintained that the present order of things is under judgement and the appropriate pattern of behaviour is rooted in the determination by whatever means possible to maintain a vision of an alternative society. Christianity has always co-existed awkwardly between these two poles.

The contrast between light and darkness sets up almost unbearable tensions for those who espouse views of separation and contradiction, whether individually or communally. If the structure of things is evil and imperils the eternal destiny of the righteous, then there is no escape from the social process except by complete separation. Of course, this is going to be more apparent than real as some social intercourse is going to be inevitable. That was recognized by the Pharisees and rabbis of Jesus' day who saw that the only way for them to be in the world but not of it was the construction of a complex network of legislation. This enabled a critical distance without being totally submerged in the dominant ideology or consigned to the complete separation of a wilderness existence like the men who wrote the Dead Sea Scrolls. But for a minority group which is fearful of its identity or dissatisfied with the *status quo* some kind of distance *is* important to assure the maintenance of the vision. The function of Revelation within the New Testament canon is to remind us of the adherence to an alternative value system (cf. Mark 10.43) in the midst of the old order, to be committed to ends rather than the endless discussion of means.

Revelation, however, refuses to allow the reader that complete certainty and satisfaction of knowing who is in the group of the elect and who is outside it. It does not countenance a simple division between the church and the world. The letters indicate that uncleanness and fornication are rife in the churches. The pollution (3.4) and nakedness which are later threats (14.4; 16.15; 17.16) are already to be found in the churches. There are no grounds for complacency, only watchfulness (3.3) and the endeavour to keep one's robes clean (22.14) so as to be found among the elect (7.14). The message is clear with regard to Babylon: 'Come out from among her, my people' (18.4), but there is little suggestion that the present practice of the church is anything but confused and compromised. The only mark of true religion is based on a prophetic witness which refuses to accept the mark of the Beast. *That* is the criterion for one's inclusion in the book of life, not membership of the Christian church or being a pillar of society.

That sharp division is evident in another area. More than any book in the New Testament, Revelation speaks of heaven. We are offered visions of its character and its inhabitants, and we may find ourselves asking about its significance. Perhaps the answer to that seems obvious: is not the destiny of humanity to be in heaven with God? That is not the answer that Revelation gives. As we shall see in our discussion of chs. 20–21, heaven ceases to be of much importance in the new age. God is *on earth*, tabernacling there with men and women (21.3). If life in the new age is our goal, therefore, what is the point of heaven?

An answer to that question is offered by Oscar, a Nicaraguan peasant, who reminds us that heaven is not a place of escape:

> There's no point in talking about heaven, wanting now to go up to heaven to see what kind of place it is; I think we've got enough on our hands to see what kind of a place the earth is . . . when people love each other there's a community of love, and that's heaven: where there's no divisions, no selfishness, where there's no deceit, that's where heaven is, that *is* heaven, that's glory.[16]

Heaven offers that alternative 'space' for God throughout most of the book. That is the place where God is acknowledged. In heaven God's ways are acknowledged consistently. It is a place where evil is *seen* to have been dealt with (12.7). For that reason heaven is a realm which presents a threat to all those who would seek to conduct their affairs according to their own criteria and in their own interests (13.6). It is a reproach to commonsense and the satisfying way of carrying on. After all, heaven cannot be seen, except by the visionary's privileged glimpse through what is normally a closed door (4.1). Unrepentant humanity needs to get rid of those who dare to remind them of another reality and another way (11.7).

In the present age heaven stands over against earth. That is not

[16] From *The Gospel in Solentiname*, ed. Ernesto Cardenal, vol. 3, Orbis Books 1984, p. 25.

part of the permanent order of things. God wishes to walk again in paradise in the cool of the day and tend the garden of the created world. The present reality is different. Revelation does not pause to explain how this reality of rebellion and injustice came about; it accepts it as a fact. In the book we are presented with difference and separation, rebellion and opposition. God is hidden and not manifest. An apocalypse is needed to make God known. The door is normally shut; the scroll of God's purposes apparently sealed. It takes the open door to lay bare something of the divine mystery. Heaven as God's dwelling speaks of an alternative dimension and perspective on reality, of God's involvement rather than (as would seem to be the case) God's absence from a world in which the nations trample the holy city (11.2).

Another consequence of viewing the world in such stark terms is the denouncing of one's opponents: the dogs, the fornicators, the unclean, the worshippers of the Beast stand as the opposite of all that is acceptable in the eyes of God and therefore of the writer. Paradoxically, in Revelation that which is opposed is often most like God: a city (ch. 17, cf. ch. 21), a Beast bearing the marks of slaughter (ch. 5, cf. ch. 13), a prophetic spirit (ch. 2, cf. 11.5 and 19.11), sexual impurity and virginity (chs. 2 and 17; cf. chs. 14 and 21), the above compared with the below (ch. 21, cf. ch. 17). This is not a total rejection, therefore. These things are a distortion of what is good. The world is not to be rejected; its wealth is not evil. It is the way in which the wealth is made that is the problem, and the disfiguration of humanity which goes in that process. Ultimately, the wealth of the nations is brought into the new Jerusalem as an entirely fitting part of the new age when it is related to the divine purpose. There is no Manichean rejection of the material world as inherently evil, nor is there any suggestion that rejection means refusal to come to terms with the hidden and threatening parts of oneself and the world as a means of distancing oneself from reality. That which is evil and to be rejected is the distortion of that which is good which masquerades as good and beneficial: its characteristic in ch. 13 is its blasphemy.

The Gospel of John, Daniel and Revelation

Two biblical texts are often juxtaposed with Revelation, though for different reasons. The Gospel of John at first sight seems a strange companion to Revelation because its form and content are so markedly different. It has been linked with Revelation almost entirely because Christian tradition asserts common authorship for the two works.[17] Linguistically it is difficult to see much of a case for that, though the tradition that John the son of Zebedee ended his life in Ephesus offers an important connection with Revelation's setting in Asia Minor. All we know about the writer of Revelation is that his name was John and that he had knowledge of the churches in Asia Minor. John's authority was not that of an apostle but of a visionary and prophet. The book of Daniel is the other biblical apocalypse and provides an interesting comparison of style while retaining a similarity of outlook which puts these two books in a category of their own in the Bible.

The Gospel of John is apparently the least apocalyptic document in the New Testament. It has frequently been regarded as an example of that type of Christianity which firmly rejected apocalyptic.[18] By that is meant that there is no imminent expectation of the end but rather the necessity of preparation for an unexpected and uncertain future. Given that apocalyptic is so often equated with the imminent expectation of the end, it is not surprising that the Gospel is sometimes viewed as a reaction against apocalyptic. We can now see the relationship between the Gospel of John and apocalyptic in a new light if we approach in the way suggested already: how does the Gospel of John fit in with the quest for higher wisdom through revelation (see above p.19)?

When viewed from this perspective, the main direction of its message appears to have a remarkable affinity with apocalyptic. Admittedly, the mode of revelation stressed in the Gospel differs from that outlined in the apocalypses. The goal of apocalyptic is the attainment of knowledge of the divine mysteries, and in particular the mysteries of God; it can be seen that much of what the Fourth Gospel says relates to this theme. Jesus proclaims himself as the revelation of the hidden God. He tells Philip, 'Anyone who has seen me has seen the Father' (14.8) and at the conclusion of the Prologue, the Evangelist speaks of the Son in the following way: 'No one has ever seen God; God's only Son, he who is nearest to the Father's heart, has made him known' (1.18). The vision of God, the heart of the call-experiences of Isaiah and Ezekiel and the goal of the heavenly ascents of the apocalyptic seers, is in the Fourth Gospel

[17] See e.g. M. Hengel, *The Johannine Question*, ET SCM Press 1989.
[18] See e.g. C.K. Barrett, *The Gospel of John and Judaism*, SPCK 1975.

embodied in the revelation of God in Jesus. All claims to have seen God in the past are repudiated; the Jews are told: 'His voice you have never heard, his form you have never seen' (5.37). Even when, as in Isaiah's case, scripture teaches that a prophet glimpsed God enthroned in glory, this vision is interpreted in the Gospel as a vision of the pre-existent Christ (12.41). No one has seen God except the one who is from God; he has seen the Father (6.46). The vision of God reserved in the book of Revelation for the fortunate seer (4.1) and for the inhabitants of the new Jerusalem who will see God face to face (Rev. 22.4) is found, according to the Fourth Evangelist, in the person of Jesus of Nazareth. Possibly an attempt is made to repudiate the claims of those apocalyptists who gained divine knowledge by means of heavenly ascents to God's throne when Jesus says to Nicodemus: 'No one has gone up into heaven except the one who came down from heaven, the Son of Man'. . . . (3.13). For the Fourth Evangelist, the quest for the highest wisdom of all, the knowledge of God, comes not through the information disclosed in visions and revelations but through the Word become flesh, Jesus of Nazareth. Thus while the Fourth Evangelist sets himself resolutely against any claim to revelation except through Christ, there is presupposed a claim to revelation with so many affinities with Revelation.[19]

A comparison between the two biblical apocalypses is instructive as much for the differences between them as the similarities. Both focus on the culmination of God's purposes and the triumph of God's faithful people, so are eschatologically orientated. In certain visions Revelation is clearly indebted to Daniel (e.g. Dan. 10 in 1.13ff.; Dan. 7 in chs. 13 and 17). Most would concede, however, that, unlike Revelation Daniel is pseudonymous, i.e. it was written in the second century BC but projected back into a fictitious setting during the exile in Babylon. There is little to suggest that as a whole or in part Revelation was written by any one other than John. There are none of the conventional trappings of pseudonymity such as a fictitious setting and authenticating claims, such as apostleship (look at II Peter for examples of these). John's authority resides primarily in his prophetic call (1.9ff.). Commentators suppose that the lack of pseudonymity in Revelation is explained by the conviction prevalent in early Christianity that the new age had seen the return of the

---

[19] These issues are explored in J. Ashton, *Understanding the Fourth Gospel*, OUP 1991, pp. 381ff.

prophetic spirit and that the need to claim authority by cloaking visions in the garb of revelations vouchsafed to ancient worthies is no longer necessary. To this extent, despite its title (1.1), Revelation does differ in its self-presentation. It is *prophecy* which manifests itself in apocalyptic form. It is the prophetic witness that is extolled and the self-conscious link with the prophets that characterizes the book.

That in part explains the absence in Revelation of one of Daniel's characteristic features: the tales about the activities of the visionary. We are treated in 1.9 to a minimum of personal detail. Why he was on Patmos, what relationship he had hitherto with the various churches and what exactly the situation of the churches was we are left to surmise from the fragmentary information offered. The absence of such stories from Revelation, however understandable, has the effect of heightening the impact of the visionary message. There is little to detract from the sense of 'something from beyond' which confronts us in Revelation.

Also, the form of the visions differs. The dream-vision followed by interpretation is almost completely lacking (Rev. 17 is a solitary exception, where contemporary historical connections are most explicitly made). It is not that the meaning of the visions is without ambiguity, as we have seen, but the immediacy of the impact of the symbolism is much more apparent. Instead of the arcane symbolism of Dan. 8-10 and the ambiguous hints of the Maccabean history we are treated in Revelation to a more graphic presentation whose import is less specific and of wider applicability, even if the precise relationship to historical circumstances, past present and future, is much more obscure. The subtle differences in form deserve our attention and suggest at least that the two centuries which separate the apocalypses and the different historical settings offer evidence of a development in the apocalyptic tradition.

What is most striking about Daniel, however, is that a significant part of the book has to do with the royal court in Babylon, and ch. 2 offers an interpretation of Nebuchadnezzar's dream. There is little evidence here of that scene so evocatively conjured up by Ps. 137 of a people dispirited, alienated by the rivers of Babylon. The picture we are offered is of men who are comfortable, cosmopolitan Jews who have a good reputation in the land of their exile. That is not to deny the nostalgia for Zion (Daniel prays facing towards Jerusalem in Dan.

6.10) and the severe limits on what the Jews described in these stories are prepared to engage in. As in Revelation, idolatry is the problem. The fiery furnace and the lions' den are the consequence for those who refuse to conform entirely. Yet there is evidence of admiration on the part of the king and a reluctance to see these significant courtiers die. The mighty pagan king Nebuchadnezzar is depicted with sympathy (unlike Belshazzar in Dan. 4). He is trapped in a system from which it is impossible to escape. Those who resist the imperial system are prepared to face suffering but have miraculous escapes. This represents quite a contrast with Revelation, where persecution is expected to include suffering (2.11; 6.9; 7.14; 11.7; 13.10; 12.11). There is promise of vindication (11.7f.) but a clear recognition that there can be no escape from the great tribulation (7.14). Vindication follows only after suffering and death. John and his circle are not close to any imperial court and are not called on to interpret royal dreams. Revelation is the apocalyptic literature of the alien and outsider, not of the wise foreigner with a privileged position at court.

It is in the portrayal and relationship with the powerful that Revelation contrasts so much with Daniel. We know nothing about John's situation. It is not impossible that he was well connected, hence his exile. We know that some in the imperial court had been exiled for their atheism in Domitian's time.[20] Even if John were socially well placed, there is a more distanced and antagonistic attitude to the politically powerful. Notwithstanding the fact that Rev. 18 reflects on Babylon's fall from the perspective of the kings, the mighty and the merchants, the position is one of vigorous rejection of all that is made of power and of thinly disguised satisfaction at the ultimate triumph of God's righteousness (14.11; 19.3). Daniel presents individuals who are immersed in the life of the pagan court with all the compromises that must have involved. Revelation seems to countenance no such accommodation. The only strategies are resistance and withdrawal (18.4). There is no space for any creative dialogue or principled accommodation in which the mighty might hear and be converted. There is little sign of the sympathetic pagan *positively* amazed at the wisdom of the Jew, the protection afforded by the Jewish God or the might of God's acts. The only reactions countenanced by Revelation are of awe (6.15 and

---

[20] Dio Cassius, *Histories* 67.14; cf. 68.1.

11.10) and anger at God (6.10; 9.20). Daniel represents the use of the apocalyptic tradition to explore a rather different religious strategy as compared with Revelation, which commends distance from anything which would impair allegiance to God the Creator.[21]

---

[21] On the theology of Revelation and its relation to the apocalyptic tradition, see R. Bauckham, *The Theology of the Book of Revelation*, CUP 1993.

Chapter 6

Chapter 12

Chapter 17

Chapter 21

COMMENTARY

The Revelation of the Risen Christ
1

The status of this book is special because it is *revelation*. To read its contents, but particularly to heed them, is to be blessed. The opening and closing words (22.18) indicate its importance. This is no mere collection of opinions but has the status of the divine word. Here for the first time is a Christian text which comes close to portraying itself as sacred scripture on a par with the writings of the old covenant.

It is from the opening words of the book that we get the word apocalyptic which we use to describe a whole type of literature. Most of the Jewish apocalypses roughly contemporary with Revelation do not describe themselves as apocalypses. Even in Revelation it is a word hardly used: John prefers to see his writing as prophecy and therefore in continuity with the Old Testament inspired word.

The dramatic opening grounds the book in *the* apocalyptic event: the revelation of God in Jesus Christ. Throughout the New Testament the words 'reveal' and 'revelation' are used of revelations vouchsafed to the saints (I Cor. 14.26) or elsewhere of experiences of the apostle Paul (II Cor. 12.2). Paul uses them of the final appearance of Christ (I Cor. 1.7) and of the most important event in his life (Gal. 1.12), the vision of Christ which changed the direction of his life. They are used by Paul to speak of the revelation of salvation in justice and judgement in Rom. 1.16ff. This terminology is a clear reminder, therefore, that New Testament writers want to signal something of demanding and devastating significance bursting over the horizon of human experience. That is the way in which Paul speaks of the Cross in I Cor. 1–3. It is folly to incomprehending humanity, but those who have eyes to see can understand it as the means of God's ultimate saving purposes. Apocalypse demands a break in our present way of looking at things. It offers an alternative perspective. That involves the recipient in witness (a favourite theme of Revelation). In this John and all other witnesses follow on from the archetypal witness, Jesus (1.5 and 3.14). The book of Revelation like the Gospel of John makes great play on the importance of a witness begun in Jesus and continued in the disciples (John 15.27). In John the story, rather than the drama of apocalyptic symbolism, constitutes that revelation. The Gospel of John could easily have been given the same title as the book of Revelation, for its message is consistently that, focussed as it is on the person of Jesus, the Word made flesh (see above p.50).

Despite its message from beyond there is a familiar greeting similar to those found in Paul's letters (1.4). As we shall see, John is not commissioned to write some abstract collection of eschatological predictions. The message is rooted in the needs and obligations of specific communities. The fact that they are in Asia (1.4) reminds us of the importance of hope and prophecy in that region in the first hundred years or so of the church's existence. In Phrygia in the second half of the second century AD Montanism, a revival movement which claimed the inspiration of the prophetic spirit, was to challenge the church to renew its zeal.[1]

The character of the God who is revealed is one who is eternally present (1.4) and who is understood in terms of the activity of Jesus and the presence of the Spirit (cf. the similar trinitarian juxtaposition in Rev. 5). Speaking of God elicits from John this kind of threefold language. It is rooted in the decisive revelation of God in Jesus. It is he who loved and washed us; it is his death which enables the decisive break in the history of humanity to take place and judgement and salvation to begin (5.5).

Like I Peter 2.5 and 9, John's view of priesthood and kingship is inclusive. All who are part of God's people share this role; it is not confined to a priestly élite or royal dynasty. This insight with regard to priesthood is not something that is new to Christianity. At the heart of Pharisaism lay the belief that God called *all* the people to holiness, so that lay people were expected to maintain the same level of holiness as the priests who ministered in the temple. It is probably from these ideas that New Testament writers developed their understanding of the people of God as a priesthood. As we shall see, in the messianic age the elect share with Christ the task of reigning (cf. Matt. 19.28).

The claim in 1.7 that all peoples of the world will lament seems to be outrageous when viewed from the perspective of isolated (and in some cases, for example at Smyrna) weak communities. These words remind them of the significance of their position. They are the

---

[1] See e.g. Eusebius, *Ecclesiastical History* V, 16ff.

ones who, despite their lowliness, may be destined to share in the messianic governance. Similarly, the crucified Messiah whose death seemed to be another sad episode in the story of Judaism and of the world is the one whose way will ultimately be vindicated (1.7). It will be then that God will be recognized as Creator and Lord of the universe (1.8).

At the start of John's vision Christ commissions him. The description draws on Old Testament passages. First and foremost, it is the moment when John receives authority from Christ himself to act as the agent of that message of doom and encouragement for the Christians in Asia Minor. Secondly, we may observe where it is that John has his vision. It comes not in some holy place in the midst of lavish divine service, but in a place of exile, albeit when John would recall the Risen Christ on the day of resurrection (Lord's day, 1.10). The prophet Ezekiel before him had seen God in exile in Babylon, far removed from the ark in the holy place of Israel, the temple in Jerusalem, and Jesus had seen the heavens open and the Spirit of God descending upon him in the wilderness (Mark 1.10). God appears to one of the suffering and oppressed people at a time of personal tribulation. It is that kind of God that Revelation (and for that matter the rest of the Bible) tells us about: a God who identifies with Hebrew slaves, a humiliated people in exile in Babylon, a crucified Messiah, an exiled Christian. In a place of isolation and exile, therefore, John meets Christ. It is a special place and moment. It is on the Lord's day that the Spirit comes upon John (cf. 4.2), probably a moment of mystical ecstasy in which he could stand outside himself and his world and see things differently. A voice tells him to write. Like Enoch, who, according to Jewish legend (see the important Jewish apocalypse I Enoch 12–15) was the heavenly scribe, John is given the task of being the divine envoy to the seven churches.

In 1.12 John talks of seeing the voice. This curious juxtaposition is typical of Revelation (cf. the Lion of Judah which turns out to be a lamb in 5.6). It stops the readers in their tracks. We hear voices; they are not to be seen. Of course, it is not to be taken literally, but the words do remind us of the engagement of all the sense of the visionary: he sees, hears, weeps, even smells (see further on ch. 4). This is not merely an encounter of the head but of the heart, indeed of the whole person, hence the way in which feelings and sense are spoken of in this apparently confused way. This is exactly what we should expect as the whole of our being confronts the living Christ.

The figure standing in the midst of the lampstand is a human figure (1.13). There is similarity with the phrase Son of Man frequently used by Jesus of himself in all the gospels (this is not immediately apparent in REB, which translates 'one like a son of man' by 'like a man'). The weak human figure who must suffer many things (Mark 8.31) and had nowhere to lay his head (Luke 9.58) is none other than the one who would come with clouds (1.7, cf. Mark 13.26) and would exercise judgement (19.11ff., cf. Matt. 25.31ff.). Yet he is no remote judge before whom the nations will cringe in the future. John sees the Risen Christ now standing in the midst of the lamps which symbolize the Christian communities (1.20). This revelation of the presence of Christ (he is one who *is*, the firstborn from the dead) is a telling reminder that the present activity of the churches is under his watchful gaze. Every word and action is of significance; there is nothing of which one might say, 'It doesn't really matter.' As the churches are to be reminded in the letters, the sort of life one lived in all its detail *does* matter. There was a distinctive pattern of behaviour and witness which needed to be adhered to. Christ appears as judge of churches (1.16) and nations (19.15). He searches the hearts and minds of those who follow him (cf. Heb. 4.12).

The presence of one who so resembles God means death (1.17). After all, who can see the face of the Lord and live (Ex. 33.20)? But this is Christ, the one who makes God known (cf. John 1.18). The touch of reassurance and the word of comfort ('Do not be afraid' ... 1.17) are the words of one who comes to be seen as the embodiment of the character and person of the invisible God (cf. Col. 1.15).

Notice the way in which important themes which are alluded to later in the vision are here enunciated. Jesus is the faithful witness (1.5). Witness (*marturia*) is not just the role of those who die for their faith. It is the obligation of all to give their lives as a testimony before the world, following the example of the true and faithful witness. The characteristics of the Risen Christ (1.18) form the basis of the messages to the angels of the seven churches (e.g. 2.1; 2.12). The sword is a sign of judgement (cf. Isa. 11.4) of one who is not an absent lord. It is a characteristic of the book of Revelation that we are not allowed to be so overwhelmed by the vision of a new world and the judgement that must precede it that we ignore that there is intimate contact and concern for the way in which the churches conduct their lives. This matters not only as far as the ultimate destiny of

Christians is concerned but also because they are integral to God's purposes in bearing witness to the Lamb who was slain.

John is commanded to write down what he has seen (1.19): 'what is now and what is to take place hereafter' (cf. 4.1). This twofold character of the revelation is important for our approach to Revelation as a whole. The revelation does not purport to be solely about the end of the age. What actually follows is a revelation of the nature of the churches and, in chs. 4–5, a vision of heaven. This parallels what we find in 4.1 where a similar phrase occurs. In 1.1 and 22.7 'what must be soon' characterizes the content of the vision and may refer to the imminent expectation of the end of the age, but more likely concerns the imminence (indeed reality) of the *presence* of the whole eschatological process in the midst of which the readers need to be aware that they are now standing

Some of what follows is past history (e.g. the death of Christ and his exaltation in ch. 5). At least that is true of the perspective of those on earth. But John's vision brings together the mind of God and human history. This is the problem of seeking to portray the relationship between the one who was, is and is to come and what is now the case, between eternity and the finite. Human chronology is not that of the apocalyptic mind. The perspective of the apocalypse, rooted as it is in the mystery of God's purposes, cannot be tied down to a particular time scale. The reality of the significance of Christ's death at a particular point in human history is immediately present with God and a fact which is true always. That is why John sees the Lamb's exaltation as if it were something that was just taking place. The coming one is one who now stands in the midst of the world as a challenger and a comforter. He demands that the mystery of that presence be heeded, particularly by those who acknowledge him as ruler of the kings of the earth (1.5). Of course, we always want to know where we can recognize that presence. If John's experience is anything to go by, it will be in places of exile, in unexpected moments with those whose words and deeds make them marginal to the processes of a world that is passing away. But John's vision will also remind us that the presence of Christ in judgement in our world is to be noted, not only in personal reprimand but in the stunning condemnation of recalcitrant humanity evident in the comprehensive manifestation of divine wrath.

The letters to the angels of the seven churches
2–3

An interesting feature of Revelation is the way in which the tremendous drama of human history told in much of the book is sandwiched between letters to the angels of the seven churches (chs. 2–3 and 22). We note that the sevenfold address is to the *angels* rather than the churches. There are two important aspects to this. Firstly, we note the exalted role bestowed on John. A human being is given a role on a par with and even more exalted than that of the angels, something John has to be reminded of later in the book (19.10, cf. 22.8). Secondly, the angels are most probably the angelic representatives of the churches, though some have argued that angel here is merely the equivalent to a church official. Apocalyptic writers were familiar with the idea that there were heavenly representatives for individuals, groups and nations (cf. Dan. 10.20f.). The message is a telling reminder that collectively the activity of individuals and churches is no ordinary matter. It is somehow embodied in the *alter ego* of the church watched over by Christ. Nothing escapes the notice of the all-seeing one (2.23; cf. 1.14; 5.6). Apparently ordinary acts are subject to critical scrutiny. Religion extends to all parts of life and the status of the church in heaven is tied up with the way its various members behave on earth. At the start of the story of God's purposes for the universe is a direct challenge to the churches by means of an incisive analysis of what the Spirit says to the churches. It is a contemporary message directed to their situation. Ancient historians have shown that there is an abundance of allusions to the local characteristics of each of the cities in each letter.[1]

The references in the letters indicate detailed local knowledge. Thus, for example, the reference in 3.18 to eye ointment is widely believed to refer to Laodicean medicine which was used for eye

---

[1] See John Sweet, *Revelation* (SCM Pelican Commentary), SCM Press 1979, and C. J. Hemer, *The Letters to the Seven Churches of Asia in their Local Setting* (JSNT Supplement Series 11), Sheffield 1986.

disorders, and the title given to Christ is reminiscent of Col. 1.15 (Colossians is adjacent to the city of Laodicea and there was close contact between the churches – see Col. 4.16). Also the wealth of the Laodiceans was legendary (3.17). After an earthquake in 61 it refused financial assistance with rebuilding. If such local issues do colour the message of Christ to the churches, we find here a theme touched on throughout the letters: the close link between religion and culture. It is expected that the Christians in Laodicea will have imbibed the dominant ethos of the place in which they live, and so their outlook will be more governed by that than by Christ. The message of the Risen Christ, then as today, is directed to particular situations and experiences. These colour the content of the message, which is direct and forceful because of that – quite a challenge to us to remember that the message of Christ is no set of timeless truths but is applied and coloured by the situations and experiences of each generation.

The letters to the seven churches each pick up on aspects of the call vision or the character of Christ in their introductions. There is some connection between the characteristics chosen and the particular situations of the churches concerned. Ephesus is addressed by the one who holds the seven stars and walks among the seven lamps. That feature of presence and the privilege of possession speaks of the reality of Christ's presence and reinforces the threat in 2.5 to remove the lamp from its place. There may be a hint that Ephesus, like Babylon later in the vision, will be thrown down from its pre-eminent position (2.5, cf. Isa. 14.14). The address in 3.1 comes from one who has the seven stars. It is a message of reproach in this case also. Both churches seem unable to realise their full potential. Ephesus has lost its first love (2.4), whereas Sardis has not brought any work to completion (3.2).

Two churches, Smyrna and Philadelphia, receive unequivocally positive addresses. These come from a Christ whose resurrection is a source of hope (2.8) and who has the messianic key (3.7). The world's assessment of Smyrna, like that of the crucified Messiah, needs to be placed in the context of the resurrection and vindication of Christ which will be ultimately manifest to the whole world (1.7). The Philadelphians and the Smyrneans are under persecution from the synagogue of Satan (2.9; 3.9). The former are told that they have the messianic key which will unlock the way to the kingdom of God. There is an open door before them (contrasting with the door shutting out the present Christ in the case of the complacent Laodiceans: 3.20).

The note of judgement is conveyed in the message to Pergamon. The sharp two-edged sword smites the nations (19.15, cf. 2.16). It is a drawn sword in the hand of the angel which is eventually seen by Balaam (Num. 22.32), so the hope is that those who follow in Balaam's footsteps will come to their senses (2.14). In the letter to Thyatira Christ appears as Son of God (a unique reference in Revelation) with eyes like flames of fire and feet like bronze. The eyes of Christ are the ever searching Spirit of God sent out into the world (5.6), which will equip him to exercise judgement (19.11f.), to be 'a searcher of hearts and minds' and to know 'the deep secrets of Satan' (2.23f.). The feet of bronze are those which tread the winepress of the wrath of God. The searching Spirit of God probes and tests the Christians at Sardis and brings to mind the teaching which they have received (cf. John 14.26) so that they may observe it (3.3). Standing over against the most backsliding of all the churches is one who is the true witness (3.14). As the one who is the agent of creation (3.14, cf. Col. 1.15), he stands apart from and superior to all human persons and institutions and demands complete allegiance and a distinctive, perhaps costly, witness, such as that which has sometimes been evident in other churches (cf. 2.13).

Just as the letters are closely linked with Rev. 1.13ff. in the introductions, so too the content of the letters not only ties in with the detail of the apocalypse proper but also indicates that present behaviour determines eschatological standing. What goes on *here and now* is therefore intimately related to the eschatological drama which follows. It is apparent that some of the circumstances in which the communities find themselves are those hinted at later in the book. Throughout the letters the importance of good works is stressed (2.2, 5, 19, 22f., 26; 3.1f., 8, 15). It is works which will be the criterion of judgement (18.6 and 20.12). The need to repent is demanded (2.16; 2.21f.; 3.3), just as it should have been the appropriate response of humanity in the face of the demonstration of divine wrath (9.20). The eschatological tribulation which is to afflict the world and cause suffering to the elect is already apparent (2.9; 2.22), though the time of testing may for some lie in the future (3.10). The characteristic way of dealing with this period, faithful endurance (14.12) is repeated (2.3; 2.19; 3.10), and the activity of witness already started (2.13; 3.14, cf. 11.1ff.) Satan is already active in the world (2.10, 12f.; cf. 12.7ff.), and the lot of the elect mentioned in 13.8 is already experienced (2.10). The threats are similar. Jezebel resembles Babylon in encouraging fornication (2.20). There is the risk of pollution (3.4, cf. 14.4) and the threat of nakedness hangs over unrepentant churches (3.17, cf. 16.15 and 17.16). The promises are those mentioned later in the book: sharing in the tree of life (2.7, cf. 22.4); escape from the second death (2.11, cf. 20.14); holding fast to my cause (2.13, 17; cf. 14.12; 21.2 and 22.4); becoming a pillar (3.12, cf. 21.24); sharing in the messianic reign (2.27; 3.21, cf. 12.5; 19.15; 20.4, and 5.10 where they already exercise that); the messianic meal ('the hidden manna' 2.17, cf. 19.9 and 3.20, where it is already a present possibility); wearing white robes (3.4, 10, 16, cf. 6.11 and 7.9) and a place in the book of life (3.5, cf. 13.8; 17.8; 20.12). The Christ of the letters is one who searches the inner being like the eschatological judge who is God's word (2.23, cf. 19.11 and Heb. 4.12), who wages war with the sword (2.16, cf. 19.11) and is David's key (3.7, cf. 5.5).

What the churches are shown is an open door to eschatological reality as a present possibility and event. An open door stands before the Philadelphian church (3.8), just as it stands before John in 4.1. That enables the reader to see what must be 'after this'. They must take care that they do not shut out the present Christ who comes as a thief, not only to wind up this present age (16.15, cf. 1.3) but to search out the lives of Christians (2.16, 25; 3.11). The demand to act in a way appropriate for those who are children of light is therefore imperative, for the eschatological drama is shown to have begun. Otherwise those who are privileged to 'be in the know' may find Christ outside the door. Heaven may then be shut to them and the insight offered squandered.

Contrasting characteristics in the messages to the churches

Positive	Negative
Ephesus	
(a) endurance	(a) loss of first love
(b) not putting up with evil men	
(c) testing false prophets	
Smyrna	
(a) tribulation, poverty	
(b) rich	
(c) endured blasphemy of so-called Jews	

Pergamum

(a) holding Christ's name
and not denying faith

(a) holding teaching of Balaam

(b) eating food sacrificed to idols
(c) holding teaching of
Nicolaitans

Thyatira

(a) love, faith, service

(a) teaching of Jezebel
(b) food sacrificed to idols

Sardis

(a) few who have not polluted
robes

(a) reputation of being alive yet
dead
(b) works not fulfilled before God

Philadelphia

(a) open door
(b) keeping God's word

Laodicea

(a) neither hot nor cold
(b) in reality poor
(c) Christ stands outside door

From this list it will be seen that there are positive things said about
six of the churches. It is all too easy to focus on what is wrong with
the churches and lose sight of the positive and affirming aspects of
the divine judgement of them. Thus in the letter to Ephesus their toil
and endurance and rejection of false apostles are commended (2.2).
There is appreciation of the tribulation and poverty of the church at
Smyrna and encouragement not to fear. Those at Pergamum are
congratulated for holding to the name (2.13). The Thyatirans' faithfulness and service as well as their improvement are noted (2.18).
Even Sardis, which is in receipt of a negative letter, can take comfort
from the fact that it has a 'few people who have not polluted their
clothing' (3.4). The weakness of the Philadelphians does not
diminish the fact that they have exhibited endurance (3.10). Even the
most negative letter of all to the Laodiceans, which has nothing by
way of a congratulatory note, indicates the love of Christ for them

(3.19) and the reality of the present Christ waiting to sup with them (3.20).

Such a mixture of encouraging comment as well as searching criticism and thorough exhortation are essential prerequisites of the pastoral practice which is grounded in Christ. There may be times, as in the letter to the Laodiceans, where, in the starkest way possible, the need to be challenged, and to see the distortions of one's way of life, is a priority. Most of the time however, all of us are that mixture of faithfulness and folly which is accurately represented in most of the other letters. We need to give each other from time to time a word of encouragement. For a variety of reasons that process of affirmation is one that we find difficult; it is much easier to find fault. All that may say much about our own sense of inadequacy and our lack of self-esteem, that we cannot easily find it in ourselves to affirm others. Indeed, often when we receive affirmation we can find ourselves distrusting what we receive and wondering about the sincerity of the donor. What is offered in the letters, therefore, represents a pattern of affirmation and correction, challenge and comfort, supporting the weak and challenging the complacent, which is the foundation of our pastoral and preaching ministry.

In the letter to Ephesus we have a picture of a church which has become complacent, having lost its first love (2.4). That lack of enthusiasm is balanced by an unwillingness to tolerate false apostles (a recurring problem in early Christianity – see II Cor. 11.12ff.). There is a similar problem in 2.20 over how to assess true and false prophecy. The gift of inspired utterance of powerful speech always makes an impression. Such charisma is not the test of the true prophet, however. The implicit test (as in Matt. 7.20) is that 'you will recognize them by their fruit'. We have no knowledge of what the practices of the Nicolaitans may have been, but we surmise that it involved compromise and lack of that distinctive cutting edge to discipleship which is so central in Revelation (cf. 2.14). We should take care not to assume that there is any condemnation of the prophecy of Jezebel because she is a woman. Prophecy among women was common in the early church (cf. I Cor. 11.5 and Acts 21.9), and Phrygia (the area in which Laodicea is situated) was the area where there was a significant prophetic movement, Montanism, about one hundred years later (see above p.58).

The church in Smyrna, by contrast, has the appearance of weakness but in God's eyes is rich. That is the measure of God's wisdom which is foolishness to humanity (see I Cor. 1.25). There was a struggle with rival Jewish congregations (Rev. 2.9; 3.9). We must remember that most of the Christians in the New Testament times thought of themselves as Jews: those Jews who did not accept Jesus as Messiah were considered by the Christians as rebelling against God. In the letter to the Philadelphians there appears to have been pressure to disown the name of Jesus (3.8), something which confronted many Jewish Christians who wished to continue to worship in the synagogues after the First Jewish Revolt in AD 70. For this group there is the real prospect of harassment (2.10). That is also true of the Christians in Pergamum where Antipas has died for his faith (2.10). Satan's home is there (2.13) because it was the site of a major centre for worship of the emperor, a major force for social and political integration in the Eastern Empire. To opt out of emperor-worship was to be a non-conformist, in Roman eyes an atheist even. There are those in Pergamum who are tempted 'to eat food sacrificed to idols and to commit fornication' (2.14). The same sins threaten the life of the community in Thyatira as the result of the activity of 'Jezebel, the woman who claims to be a prophetess'. The former is a reference to an unwillingness to dissociate oneself from the regular habits of life of the ancient city. The latter is probably not to be taken literally but (as in the Old Testament) is a way of speaking about the compromise with surrounding culture and practice which renders an effective Christian witness redundant.

The churches at Sardis and Laodicea have the reputation of spiritual maturity and well-being. Such appearances are deceptive however (3.1, 16f.). Christ's assessment pierces to the heart of things (cf. Heb. 4.13: 'nothing in creation can hide from him'). The problem in Sardis is a growing forgetfulness of the demands of the gospel ('remember the teaching you received', 3.3), for it is the Spirit's task to remind Christians in every generation of the challenge of discipleship rooted in the sayings and deeds of Jesus (John 14.26). Over the centuries the church has often ignored the hard sayings of Jesus and accommodated the demands of the gospel, ending up compromised and lukewarm in the faith (3.15). In contrast the (apparently) feeble strength of the Philadelphian Christians merits warm praise and encouragement (3.8f.).

The conclusion of the letter to Laodicea offers a graphic portrait of Christ standing *outside* the community seeking to enter. 3.20 inspired the famous Holman Hunt painting 'The Light of the World'. It should be remembered that the picture here is one of exclusion by a community which thought it had Christ in its power. It is a salutary reminder that the living Christ refuses to be tied down by our ecclesiastical formulae and prejudices. It is not those who are most certain and powerful in the faith who are the ones where Christ is to be found:[2]

> Christ our companion,
>> you came not to humiliate the sinner
>> but to disturb the righteous.
>> Welcome us when we are put to shame,
>> but challenge our smugness,
>> that we may truly turn from what is evil,
>> and be freed even from our virtues,
>> in your name, Amen.[2]

[2] From Janet Morley, *All Desires Known*, enlarged ed., SPCK 1992, p. 10.

The praises of God

4

One of the features of Revelation is the way in which the images appear to suggest that God appears to be absent but in fact is a present reality in human life. In ch. 1 John had seen the way in which Christ was intimately concerned for the life of the churches. Here, in a world which seems bereft of God, John is allowed to see the reality. A door is opened in heaven and John is in the spirit (cf. 1.10 – probably a reference to a state of visionary ecstasy). John sees God enthroned in glory. The point is clear, however strange the details of the picture. God exists and is truly the Creator of the universe ('sovereign Lord of all', 4.8; 'you have created all things', v. 11). Even if another lord appears to rule the world at present, such a rule can only be temporary and must certainly be inadequate. The King of kings and Lord of lords (Rev. 19.16) is really ruler of the universe and will be seen to be such when the whole earth shall see the salvation of God. The God who appeared at the Exodus and made a covenant with Israel (Ex. 19.16) in thunder and lightning is not merely part of of Israel' s past story alone. At present that reality is only apparent to the eye of vision, but in due course the holiness of God will be apparent in all creation.

These two passages root Revelation in the prophetic and apocalyptic books of the Old Testament. Links with Daniel 7.13, 10.5, Ezek. 1.26 are to be found in 1.13ff. and to Ezek. 1, Isa. 6 and Ezek. 28.13 in Rev. 4. This passage draws on Old Testament visions of God. Like Isaiah and Ezekiel before him, John describes the holy God who seemed far removed yet ever present and active. That is a reminder that, when the prophets sought to speak of God and the mysteries of God, there was an established convention for doing so. So, even if we suppose that John was a real visionary (as I think we should), it would be a mistake to suppose that he was alone in writing about experience of the holy God of Israel. The Bible occasionally does so (Ezekiel 1 and Isaiah 6 are two good examples), and it would have been quite natural for a Jew to have been influenced by these exemplars. We know from contemporary Jewish sources that the first chapter of Ezekiel formed the central text in the Jewish mystical tradition. Mystics believed that it was possible by meditating on this text to 'see again' what had appeared to the prophet Ezekiel by the river Chebar.'[1]

We would not do justice to Revelation if we did not note the central role that worship plays in the book. The first of several hymnic passages (they may reflect the hymns of praise used in local synagogues) are to be found in ch. 4. Two things can be said about these passages, which stretch from ch. 4 to ch. 19. Firstly, the *character* of the worship indicates the complete participation of the worshippers. This involves not only words but also the whole person: 'the twenty four elders prostrate themselves before the throne ... as they *lay* their crowns before the throne' (4.10). This worship includes an important physical dimension to the expression of acknowledgement of God. It is uninhibited praise, an expression of the whole of oneself. It is a mark of the cerebral character of our faith that we can readily confine worship to verbal expressions (though we make an exception for music). Of course, music is important (cf. 14.2) and in many respects comes closest of all to the non-verbal expression to which the apocalyptic symbolism of the visions beckons us. But physical and sensory participation in worship (the smell of incense is hinted at in 8.3ff.) are important components of a complete worship of God.

Secondly, the worship of God is set in the context of acknowledgement of God in particular deeds. Hymning God the Creator demands a pattern of behaviour from worshippers who laud God thus. That manifests in particular kinds of deeds the fact that creation is God's, and humans have a due responsibility for it. Those who worship God truly will not worship without doing the works of God (cf. I John 3.17). When worship becomes an escape from life and from witness, it has lost touch with the true worship which God expects. There is always a great temptation to allow worship and church-going to be ends in themselves. With the strains of life being what they are there is a great appeal in seeing Christian activity as a haven from the rigours of normal life. Thus worship is a place to escape from the hurly-burly of existence into another world. Revelation

---

[1] See further C. Rowland, *The Open Heaven*, pp. 269ff., and G. Scholem, *Major Trends in Jewish Mysticism*, reissued Schocken Books 1974.

certainly does not support such a view. The paeans of praises are related to God's actions in history. The heavenly worship does not offer John an escape from the world but a glimpse of true acknowledgement of God which, as is made quite clear throughout the whole of the book, is manifest in particular patterns of obedience.

As we can see from the following summary of the hymnic pieces in Revelation, the verbal expression of worship of God include a variety of sentiments. It would appear that their various details offer commentary on what has been happening in the surrounding context of the vision:

4.8: God's holiness praised.
4.11: God honoured as Creator.
5.9: the Lamb's redemptive work is hailed as the basis for the opening of the seals.
5.12: the Lamb is worthy to receive the same worship as God.
5.13: the Lamb and God linked in praise.
7.10: the multitude proclaims God's and the Lamb's sovereignty.
11.15: response to the seventh trumpet after the second woe, assertion of God's sovereignty.
11.17f.: God is thanked for the demonstration of power and sovereignty in the face of the rage of the nations.
12.10: salvation belongs to God and this is exemplified in the casting out of Satan from heaven.
15.3: those who conquer the Beast praise the justice of God's works and God as Creator.
16.5f.: God is worthy; the justice of the judgement on the ones who shed the blood (cf. 16.3f.)
16.7: God is the Creator whose judgements are just and true.
19.1: Justice of God's judgements, particularly with regard to the judgement of the harlot by a vast throng.
19.3: praise by the vast throng as the smoke of the judgement of Babylon goes up.
19.4: praise of the twenty-four elders.
19.5: instruction from the throne to servants to praise God.
19.6: praise for the demonstration of God's reign with anticipation of the marriage of the Lamb.

It is noteworthy that there is no example of divine worship either in the account of the messianic reign or in the new creation. That may suggest that worship is a phenomenon of the old order. In the new age, when men and women see God face to face and God 'tabernacles' with them, they will serve God (7.15) in unmediated fashion. In the old order worship maintains the identity of those who refuse to see things as the world sees them. Their praise of God is an acknowledgement that all that there is to be seen is not all that matters, and that, despite the horror of all that is happening in the world, the wrath of God is not arbitrary and capricious, even if the inscrutability of God's ways lies beyond human comprehension.

The Lamb who was slain
5

This is the pivotal chapter in the book. The account of the opening of the seals, which in turn leads to the trumpet blasts and the pouring of the bowls of wrath, have their start here in the claiming of the right by the Lamb to open the seals. The scroll with seven seals appears to represent God's purposes for the restoration of the world which are set in train by the coming of the Messiah. The opening of the seals marks the beginning of the revelation of divine judgement on the world (chs. 6, 8–9 and 16). It is a dramatic moment. While this divine judgement ultimately is sanctioned by God and justified by the heavenly court, it is executed by agents who carry out purposes hidden long before in the sealed book. Writing has an important place in Revelation (e.g. 1.19): the key to the climax of human history is a book which is sealed (5.1), the elect are those whose names are written in the book of life (13.8) and the message to the seven churches comes in a written message commissioned by Christ and written by John. This message is therefore contractual in that it can be referred to; it is not based on hearsay. That is the essence of the covenant which is the basis of God's contract with humanity from Noah (Gen. 9.12) to Christ (Mark 14.24).

The scene in heaven in ch. 4 is taken up and transformed by the coming of a Lamb 'with the marks of sacrifice, standing with the four living creatures, between the throne and the elders' (5.6). We are left in little doubt about the identity of the Lamb: it has marks of sacrifice and is also the Messiah (5.5: 'the Lion from the tribe of Judah, the shoot growing from David's stock'). No one else is found worthy to open the seals. It is a Messiah with a difference, one who comes to the divine presence as a suppliant and with the marks of suffering. The curious Greek of 5.6, which REB translates 'Then I saw a Lamb with the marks of sacrifice on him, standing with the four living creatures between the throne and the elders', presents the Lamb as one who *stands* rather than sits (cf. Acts 7.56 and Mark 14.62). The creature comes before the divine tribunal as a suppliant and is vindicated. The description of the Lamb indicates that it is the one from whom the Spirit proceeds ('the eyes which are the seven spirits of God', cf. Acts 2.30ff. and John 14–16). Already those attributes of God described independently in 4.5 are linked with the Lamb.

What is most significant about the picture we are offered, however, is that a weak creature with no mark of triumph but the marks of its own slaughter should turn out to be the agent of God's purposes: 'we proclaim Christ nailed to the cross; and though this is an offence to Jews and folly to Gentiles, yet to those who are called, Jews and Greeks alike, he is the power of God and the wisdom of God' (I Cor. 1.23f.). Rev. 5 seems to be saying: this moment of utter defeat when a would-be Messiah died in apparent failure has turned out to be the decisive moment in history. An event of little concern to the writers of the age, when a trouble-maker received the just reward for his actions, cried out to heaven for acknowledgement. The Lamb not only receives the scroll containing God's purposes but also shares with God the worship of heaven and earth (5.12) and God's throne (7.17). That event in Palestine affected the way in which God related to the world. Just as at the moment of Jesus' death, according to the Gospel of Mark, the veil of the temple is ripped in two, symbolizing the end of the old order (Mark 15.38), so here too the symbolism speaks of Jesus' life and death making a difference to the world and God's relationship to it. God's relationship to creation could never be the same again; humanity is taken into the godhead, thus enabling those who identify with this improbable Messiah to become God's priests and to exercise the messianic reign in the future (5.10, cf. Matt. 19.28 and I Cor. 6.3). The Lamb becomes the means of bridging the gap between heaven and earth which injustice and disobedience have brought about.

The seven-horned Lamb contrasts with the Beast of ch. 13 with ten heads (13.1) and two horns like the Lamb (13.11). The Lamb, however, comes to God and is accepted by God. This is the identity of the *true* ruler of the kings of the earth, whose sovereighnty does not come by force of arms or by the exploitation of the inhabitants of the world and its resources, but by self-offering (cf. Phil. 2.5ff.). Another contrast is between the description of Christ in 1.13ff. and here. Whereas in ch. 1 Christ is described in language familiar to us from theophanies and angelophanies in the Old Testament (Ezek. 1.26; Dan. 7.13; 10.5ff.), John does not use this terminology. Rather he speaks of a pathetic creature and he chooses to speak thus of

Christ throughout the rest of the apocalypse. The distinguishing mark, therefore, is not the trappings of divine glory and power but weakness and death.

It could be that a point is being made about Christ which is of some importance. There was a tradition in Judaism of exalted, quasi-divine beings,[1] some of whom exercised divine power and were on a par with God. Perhaps some of this confusion over the status of angelic beings is evident in 19.10 where John would fall down and worship an angel, presumably because he thought it was God or Christ. John is rebuked and the position of angels is clarified: they are only fellow-servants like the human prophets. What distinguishes Christ is not the trappings of divinity which other angels share in contemporary Jewish texts (and the Risen Christ in 1.13ff. does too). Christ's suffering is what enables him, rather than any other member of the heavenly court, to be hailed as Messiah and to exercise the messianic task. Indeed, if we compare the opening chapters of Hebrews, where the issue of Christ's status *vis-à-vis* the angels is discussed, the clinching argument is not so much the application to Christ of scriptures which had been applied to God but the fact that Christ made cleansing of our sins (1.3) and then sat down at God's right hand, very much as the Lamb does in Rev. 5.

Revelation is preoccupied with holiness. The dominant characteristic of the new Jerusalem is that nothing profane will enter into it (21.27). The picture is an ambiguous one. For all the clarity of boundaries between sacred and profane, good and evil, darkness and light, right at the very centre of Revelation stands a corpse. Uncleanness is found at the very heart of God, sharing God's throne (7.17). The Lamb is dead and so a source of uncleanness (Num. 19.11ff.). That is the central paradox of the gospel. The dead Messiah is the one who, according to the letter of the Hebrews, enters not the holy place but the holiest place of all, heaven itself (Heb. 9.20ff.). The contemporary boundaries are blurred and convention and custom thrown into the melting pot. Priesthood does not any longer belong to the tribe of Levi but is according to the order of Melchizedek. Qualifications for that office are not rooted in gender or in cleanness but in faith in the one who enters the sanctuary behind the curtain, having entered on our behalf as forerunner (Heb. 6.20).

[1] See L. W. Hurtado, *One God, One Lord: Early Christian Devotion and Ancient Jewish Monotheism*, SCM Press 1988.

As compared with ch. 4, where God is hymned alone (a chapter which, as we have suggested, differs little from contemporary accounts of visions of God), ch. 5 includes the coronation of the Lamb. Of course, there must be a sense in which nothing catches God out: after all the Lamb is slain before the foundation of the world (13.8, cf. I Peter 1.20). Yet here we are treated to that moment of significance when a death brings about the climactic change in the relationship between heaven and earth. Nothing would be the same again. If we may put it so, the Lamb's sacrifice has had its effect on God too. The one who was dead is now alive and shares God's throne. The experience of human life and death is taken into God in a way that has never happened in this way before. A human being shares the intimacy of God's throne (cf. John 1.18, where the Logos is in the bosom of the father). In the language of apocalyptic we find outlined the significant moment of John 1.14 when the divine Logos took flesh. Here in Rev. 5 it is the transformation of heaven rather than humanity which is the point being made. That is done not by the storming of heaven by violence. Christ is no Prometheus who seeks to invade heaven. The secret of the heart of God and proximity to God's own person is rooted in the sacrificial death of the Lamb. The character of God is revealed in this. Paul had put it thus: 'God did not spare God's own son but gave him up for us all' (Rom. 8.32). That is the mystery of God and of the Messiah.

If it is this kind of character which merits the worship of the heavenly host, then questions have to be asked about the character of the life which is acceptable to God. For adherents of 'Christian realism', the focus on the symbol of the Lamb with marks of slaughter encourages naivety. But the uncomfortable fact is that it is not the mighty of the world who attract fame and attention, those who are worldly-wise, those who run the system best of all. It is those who are victims of the system, just as the Lamb was, who are promised the blessings of the age to come (7.16). Rev. 5 compels us consider a different understanding of the meaning of success and the exercise of power. This is so difficult for the followers of the Lamb to hold on to when all the pressures are to conform to a culture of self-aggrandizement and self-promotion. What Rev. 5 stresses is that self-offering and human weakness, recognized and accepted, is the life that is acceptable to God. It is not the glorification of self or systems which are typical of the contrasting creatures in Rev. 13 whose own self-glorification is the root of blasphemy.

In our concentration on the symbol of the Lamb we need to take care not to be enslaved by the symbol used. The striking character of the image used should not lead us to suppose that passivity is all that is encouraged thereby. The juxtaposition of the Lion of Judah and the Lamb certainly challenges our assumptions about the character of the Messiah, but that image does not by any means exhaust what John wants to tell us about Jesus. It must be complemented by passages like 1.13ff. and 19.11ff. The Lamb goes to its death not with a fatalistic acceptance of its lot. Nor is its death all that is important about it. Jesus is after all the 'faithful witness' (1.5; 3.14). He has had an *active* role in life, and, like the two witnesses in ch.11, that activity in pursuance of the witness to God led to death. That task of witness so graphically demonstrated in the account of the dialogue between Jesus and Pilate in the Gospel of John (18.33ff.) suggests no mere acceptance of death. It is testimony before the nations of that other way, the way of truth. That is what true messiahship consists of. It is that also which the writer of I Timothy gives expression to when he speaks of Jesus as having made a 'noble confession in his testimony before Pontius Pilate' (I Tim. 6.13).

We shall note throughout the apocalypse moments when John ceases to be a mere spectator of the drama that unfolds before him and becomes a participant. One such moment occurs in 5.4. Elsewhere John is instructed to write (1.19, cf. 19.9). In 7.13 he is asked about the great multitude; in 10.9ff. he is commanded to eat the scroll and prophesy. In 11. 1 he is given a measuring rod, in 17.3 he is taken to a desert place, and in 19.10 he falls down before an angel and is rebuked. In the face of what he sees, John's emotions are allowed full sway. In 5.4 his bitter grief bursts forth when it appears that there is no one to bring about justice and vindication. The outburst of sadness is a welcome and important intrusion. It is above all a *human* response in the midst of this heavenly world to complement the intensely human drama of Calvary. John's weeping is the anguish in the face of a disordered world and an expression of disappointment that things are not turning out right. Like the martyrs who long for vindication and justice in 6.9f., John needs patience and understanding of God's purposes. But John and the martyrs are not excluded from the eschatological process. The latter are given robes, signs of their ultimate vindication (cf. 3.5). John here and elsewhere has a task to perform. He is a witness of 'what must take place hereafter' (4.1). He must give an account of the perspective on the 'higher level' of the drama. In addition, he brings into the divine presence signs of weakness and sadness, something which is now known to be possible with the exaltation of the Lamb with the marks of slaughter.

Perhaps the most problematic thing about this chapter concerns its relationship to what follows. The triumph of the Lamb is followed by a demonstration of horror and disaster afflicting humankind. The gentle Lamb's exaltation and paean of praise which greets the acceptance to God's throne are followed by a dramatic new act of God which is hardly good news for the world:

> ... on to the stage of history come only four horsemen representing disasters as old as the human race. Is this all that we are to receive from the regnant Christ? Has he after all nothing new to disclose, nothing new to achieve? Indeed, we may be pardoned for asking whether the Lamb who let such horrors loose on the world is really the same person as the Jesus of the gospel story.[2]

In such sentiments (as Caird in his commentary well recognizes) there are implicit many of the prejudices concerning the book of Revelation: that it preaches a message of vengeance contrary to the spirit of the rest of the New Testament. Nevertheless there is an instinct here which cannot easily be brushed aside: doom and disaster seem to be the prominent thread which stands out in the texture of Revelation. There is hope; but it is muted and confined in its scope. We seem to be far removed from the God who so loved the world that God sent the Son into the world to save it (cf. John 3.16). Accordingly, there is a question to be asked which goes to the heart of the Judaeo-Christian religion: does God countenance, indeed, permit that which is evil in the world? We know that the Bible as a whole steadfastly refuses to countenance one solution to the problem: theological dualism. That still leaves us with passages which affirm God as Creator of both light and darkness, and ultimately the one who permits evil, even if in the end it is to be overthrown.

At the very heart of God's purposes is one who bore the full force of evil. There was done to this person all the injustice of which a chaotic creation is capable, an injustice which undergirds the apparent façade of dignity and beauty so ruthlessly unmasked in this apocalypse. The juxtaposition of Rev. 5 with Rev. 4 is a clear indication of the importance of the career of Jesus in his life and death to the divine purposes. Rev. 5 indicates that nothing could be the same again. In comparison with Rev. 6, however, ch. 5 presents the

---

[2] G. B. Caird, *The Revelation of St John the Divine*, A. & C. Black 1966, p. 82.

key for a true understanding of reality. It is that sort of life and that sort of death which have wrested the right to open the scroll and put into effect God's redemptive purposes. Rev. 5 offers an authentication of the true form of messianism. The Lion of Judah, the Root of David does not turn out to be the warrior Messiah. Instead we have the juxtaposition of messianic hope and fragile weakness in the shape of the bloody Lamb. That is the way of triumph; that is the divine way in the light of which all else is shown up in its true nature. The contrast between the two chapters shows up the difference between heaven and earth, God and the world. Just as the Lamb embodies injustice perpetrated which so disfigures the world, so its exaltation issues in a recognition of the *extent* of that injustice; there can be no proper triumph of the Lamb without a revelation of the reality of the disorder of the world. The perfect one now presents imperfection in all its awefulness.

Of course, the unfolding of woes and disasters is very much part of the fabric of Jewish eschatological expectation. Roughly speaking, we may say that Jewish expectation repudiated the notion that there was to be a gradual evolution of goodness in the world. Rather, the testimony of ancient Jewish texts is that there would be a period of tribulation which had to be endured before the reign of God finally came. That is exactly the belief that undergirds the eschatological disourses of Jesus in the synoptic gospels (Mark 13; Matt. 24–25; Luke 21) and the terse description of the agony of the created world in Rom. 8.19ff. What all these texts indicate is that messianism does not mean the immediate triumph of God over the powers of evil. There is a frank recognition of the pervasiveness and power of evil which is both endemic and consequently not easily rooted out.

Manifestations of judgement
Chapter 6, together with comments relevant to chapters 8, 9, 11.15–19 and 16

There is much overlap between these chapters which give a structure to the major part of Revelation. As will be seen from the table below, there is overlap of content. Whether we should assume that there is supposed to be some kind of chronological sequence or threefold repetition to make the point about the judgement which will affect an unjust and unrepentant world is unclear. Some have preferred to see them as a threefold repetition of the character of judgement, though there is a sense of climax in the culmination in the 'last' plagues (15.1), the intensification of judgement consequent on the trumpet blasts and the the proclamation introduced by the seventh trumpet in 11.15f. The two passages where the opening of a seal (6.9) and the blowing of a trumpet (11.19) do not lead to disasters, but to the cry for vindication and the revelation of the ark of the covenant, are reminders that the divine wrath is rooted in justice manifested in the obligations laid upon humanity. It is this kind of conviction that prompts the declaration and question of the psalmist: 'God takes his place in the court of heaven to pronounce judgement among the gods. How much longer will you judge unjustly and favour the wicked? Uphold the cause of the weak and fatherless, and see right done to the afflicted and destitute' (Psalm 82.1–3).

Trying to make sense of terror and turmoil

Readers will be aware that these passages have been a happy hunting ground for those who wish to find prophecies of cosmic and ecological disaster in scripture (thus Wormwood in 8.11 is said to be a prediction of the Chernobyl disaster). The reaction when we find contemporary events predicted in scripture is for 'sensible' Christians to reject such identification and argue that what is referred to is either only of eschatological significance or is entirely bound up with

SEALS	TRUMPETS	BOWLS
6.1–2: first horseman conquers	8.7: hail and fire mixed with blood; third of earth burnt up	16.2: evil sores appear on those with mark of Beast
6.2, 4: second horseman removes peace from the earth, so humans would slay one another	8.8–9: third of sea creatures die after burning mountain thrown into sea and latter is turned to blood	16.3: sea become blood and every living thing in its dies
6.5–6: third horseman: famine and inflated prices	8.10–11: water made bitter after star falls from heaven; people die from drinking water	16.4: river and springs become blood
6.7–8: fourth horseman: quarter of earth killed by sword, famine, death and wild beasts	8.12: third of sun does not shine nor do moon and stars	16.8–9: humans scorched by sun
6.9: martyrs plead for vindication	**THREEFOLD WOE**	16.10: darkness over the kingdom of the Beast
6.12–17: earthquake; sun darkened; stars fall from the heaven; heaven rolls up; kings and mighty hide themselves from God's presence	9.1–6: air polluted by smoke from abyss after star falls from heaven. Locusts created from smoke harm humans. Humanity tormented by insects with scorpion stings	16.12: Euphrates dried up to prepare a way for the kings of the east. Spirits from dragon, Beast and false prophet work miracles to assemble kings at Armageddon
8.1: silence in heaven followed by prayers of saints contained in the incense offering	9.13ff.: third of humanity killed after release of the angels bound at the Euphrates	16.17: earthquake which splits great city into three; every island vanishes.
	11.15–19: celestial worship proclaiming the fact that God reigns. Sanctuary in heaven opened	

what John expected in his day. Precise allusions are indeed unlikely, and we would be diminishing the ongoing significance of this passage if we said that it only had relevance to *one* specific event. Whatever the risks involved of the fevered imagination allowing precise identification, it is probably a correct instinct to suppose that the disasters of our world are not to be excluded from the pattern of God's grace and judgement. To abstract God from the complexity of social and ecological processes is to diminish the reality of the account we want to give of God's part in our world. If Revelation seems to highlight divine judgement rather than mercy, that is a message which an idolatrous generation needs to hear. If Mammon is our God, then the consequences of idolatry are manifest in the judgement to which we are consigned for our short-sighted self-interest. We live as part of an order in which injustice has distorted the way in which society and the whole created order functions. The world is out of joint, and that was most clearly demonstrated in the destruction of the Messiah by the representatives of the present scheme of things. The Messiah represents a very different scheme of values (Mark 10.43–44) which shows up the distorted and fractured nature of the world, humans, beasts and the whole of creation for what it really is. Despite all that, in its perversity humanity persists in carrying on in the same old way, ignoring the justice of God, indeed cursing the very God who can offer life and true peace and harmony (9.20; 16.9, and 11).

Revelation seems to portray death and destruction as in some sense coming from God. The sequence of seals, trumpets and bowls is initiated by the Lamb taking the heavenly book (chs. 5, 6, 8–9 and 16). Two things can be said about this. First of all, in the context of the book the wrath of God against a recalcitrant world is a stark reminder of God's justice. Evil and injustice will not always prevail. The sequence of seals, trumpets and bowls outline the predetermined evolution of the divine purposes in history as the structures of the world give way to the messianic age (the millennium). Judgement is necessary because there is no sign of repentance. God's righteousness reveals itself in judgement against humanity because of the alienation of human society from the way of God. The maintenance of that structural injustice which is unresponsive to the need for change in line with God's will results in ultimate destruction. The God of the covenant is not one who will allow the cry of the weak and the oppressed to go unheard (Ex. 3.7; cf. Gen. 4.10). The reality which the Apocalypse points us to is that in a disordered world death

83

and destruction are the lot of millions, and the putting right of wrongs demands a seismic shift of cosmic proportions which *will* happen, even if humankind does not repent.

We like our religion to be kind, gentle and non-violent, a soothing balm on our troubled world. Emotions like anger and vindictiveness are less acceptable, and we prefer to put distance between ourselves and the reality of such feelings within us. But we should remember that so-called Christian civilization has been responsible for the most brutal and dehumanizing moments in human history. May it not be that part of the problem is that the violence and harshness which we find in Revelation and echoed from time to time in other parts of the New Testament we would rather ignore, and so deny as part of the reality of ourselves and our world? Possibly it is all too close to what we are really like for comfort. A book like Revelation reminds us too much of ourselves and our attitudes, buried for the most part beneath a veneer of respectability. It may just question whether in fact we are the kind, gentle, loving religious people we like to think of ourselves and see in others.

We are rightly concerned with the preoccupation with evil and its terrible destruction in the book of Revelation. The ruthless exclusion of the representative of evil from heaven in ch. 12 and the same action against all that is unclean speaks of an abhorrence of profanity and evil which can easily lead us to suppose that there is none of that imperfection in ourselves. The letters to the seven churches are a constant reminder that evil is something that is by no means restricted to the 'secular' world. It is the determined exposure of all that is opposed to the holy God in oneself which enables Revelation to guard against advocating a 'holier than thou' attitude among its readers. In its vigorous exclusion of all that is evil it demonstrates evil's reality and demands that we come to terms with it as a present potent force. Exclusion can so easily lead to our denying it in ourselves, however. Evil too often is something that is excluded rather than being owned and overcome. Revelation demands that we recognize the dark side of ourselves and our world. It does not merely exclude that which is evil. The Beast, the False Prophet, the Dragon are all unmasked before they are excluded. Our mistake would be to suppress that dark side and exclude the possibility of its influence before we acknowledged its power in us. We must always make sure that in wrestling with the fact and overcoming of evil as it is set out in Revelation, we do not allow ourselves to be misled into supposing that mere exclusion of the Satan either from heaven or earth is enough. The power of darkness in heaven had infected the cosmos as a whole so that its redemption was necessary. There had to be a war in heaven before Satan could be overthrown (cf. 12.7); there had to be a significant death before there could be that catharsis which would prepare the cosmos for its ultimate liberation.

> O God, against whom we struggle,
> > you speak with the voice of the persecuted
> > and call the oppressor to turn to you:
> > confront in us the violence that we enact or consent to,
> > that our strength may be made perfect in weakness,
> > and we may put our trust in you,
> > through Jesus Christ, Amen.[1]

Taking God's wrath seriously

Even if we can understand something of the importance of the recognition of the darker side of the world and of ourselves, we are still faced with the issue of why it is that God countenances such aweful things to happen in the name of messianic salvation. It may be tempting to distance God from it all and say that it is not God's direct responsibility. To do that would be open the door to dualistic solutions which the Judeo-Christian tradition has always shunned. It was a major task of the early Christians to reject the beliefs of those who argued (like Marcion of Sinope) that the responsibility for evil in the world was that of some lesser divine being who created the world amiss, and that true religion meant communion with a higher divinity uncontaminated by the world of matter. However difficult it may be, Revelation (and the rest of the biblical witness for that matter) compels us to recognize God's ultimate responsibility for that which appears to us evil and destructive. In these chapters we have our noses rubbed in this problem in no uncertain terms. It is *God's* sealed book that is opened and it is *God's* Messiah who opens the seals which lead to the dreadful happenings then set out. This is none other than the wrath of the Lamb (6.16).

So the message of Revelation 6ff., with its tale of destruction and death, is not apart from God, however much we might prefer to shield God from it. Of course, there is no easy answer to the problem

---

[1] Janet Morley, *All Desires Known*, p. 7.

of suffering and pain that such divine involvement suggests. But then a theology after the horrors of Auschwitz and Hiroshima cannot escape wrestling with such human pain and the question of the reality of the divine presence in the most cataclysmic and destructive events in history. A Christian theology which does not find itself stumbling again and again on the scandal of suffering has never taken seriously the scandal of the execution of Jesus, the Word made flesh.

Let us remember that Revelation is not the sole representative of this harsh message of divine judgement. Throughout the Bible there is a message of judgement against injustice, particularly against the ignoring or perversion of God's covenant demands. From the early chapters of Genesis via the canonical prophets and the story of Israel's kingdoms, to the gospels and Pauline epistles and Revelation, the message is the same. In the light of this we should not polarize God's care and mercy and God's judgement. It is rather a sentimental view of God's love that has led to a notion of love which avoids issues of justice. Does the love of God involve an attitude of condescension, whatever the situation and irrespective of behaviour? The answer to that must be a resounding no. Assertion of the action of the love of God does not mean a bland indulgence of the *status quo* nor an anodyne inclusivenesss. It is rooted in the notion of covenant faithfulness which involves mutual responsibilities: 'If you love me, you will keep my commandments,' says the Johannine Jesus (John 14.15, cf. Deut. 30.15ff.). The manifestation of God's love is rooted in acts of salvation (1.5) and in the reciprocal acts of witness and prophecy of those who 'faced with death . . . did not cling to life' (12.11). As the writer of I John shows most clearly, the love of God is demonstrated in the death of Christ (I John 4.19, cf. Rom. 5.8). It is marked by responsive behaviour and the manifestation of that love in everyday life (I John 3). Those who refuse come under condemnation when they neglect to do this, just as what was supposed to be an elect and holy nation did in the critical denunciations of the prophets.

We need to keep the account of the exercise of wrath in tension with the story of the peaceable Messiah. The picture we are given in chs. 5 and 6 is entirely consistent with what we find elsewhere in the New Testament, albeit in less explicit form. An important passage in this respect is Rom. 1.16. In speaking of the gospel Paul includes in it the revelation of God's justice and the revelation of God's wrath. Exactly how the two passages are related is unclear, but it is a juxtaposition which is very much akin to the revelation of God's salvation and judgement in Revelation.[2] As in Revelation, so in Rom. 1, all commentators are agreed that the wrath mentioned here is God's eschatological wrath manifested against impiety and injustice, particularly evident in idolatry (see further on Rev. 13). The refusal to acknowledge God leads to a determined response from God. There is a threefold assertion that 'God has given them up' (Rom. 1.24, 26 and 28). Idolatrous behaviour leads to a perverted outlook on the world (1.21). That threefold giving up by God covers three areas: the desires of the heart, the passions of dishonour (1.26) and finally the undiscerning mind which does that which is unbecoming (there then follows a list of vices which result in disrupted and unharmonious living). Paul does not concentrate on sexual misdemeanours only in this passage, but also includes behaviour which contributes to society's malfunctioning, all of which is rooted in idolatry. In Romans it is God who consigns the impious to particularly distorted patterns of behaviour, just as in Revelation the source of judgement is in the divine book with seven seals. The cataclysmic effects may not be immediately apparent in the list of consequences in Rom. 1. What we are offered there is a prosaic description of a world marked by deceit and human selfishness. Stripped of the apocalyptic symbolism, the message is much the same as in Rev. 6 and 8–9, however. In Rev. 6.4 the second horseman removes peace from the earth, so that people slay one another: here is the consequence of the strife, envy and covetousnessness that Paul had spoken of in Rom. 1.28.

What we are not allowed to see in Revelvation is the state of the world before it is subjected to God's wrath. We may surmise that because the Lamb ended up being slaughtered and the same fate awaits the faithful witnesses to God (ch. 11), humanity exhibits little concern for God's ways and God's envoys. The death of Christ unlocks God's eternal purposes for humanity but is also a demonstration of the perverted mind and order of things that has led to the execution of God's Messiah. Humanity, caught as it is in the web of its social and individual preoccupations, is in no real position to judge; their minds are clouded (cf. Rom. 1.24) until such time as they are renewed by faith in the Messiah for divine service in the power of the Spirit (Rom. 12.1).

[2] See further G. Bornkamm, 'The Revelation of God's Wrath' in *Early Christian Experience*, ET SCM Press 1969, pp. 47ff.

Despite the universal and indiscriminate effects of the judgement as the seals are opened, the reactions of particular groups are highlighted. The opening of the fifth seal focusses on the martyrs (6.9). The cry for vindication and vengeance is an understandable one. We do well not to despise this honest expression of desire which lies deep within each one of us and which can spring out should the opportunity arise. God's response to them is comfort and an exhortation to patience. The witness (and death) of others has to take place first. That may seem a rather lukewarm response. Yet it is a reminder of the important task of witness. That cannot be bypassed; it must go ahead; humanity has to be given the opportunity to listen and see things differently. There is, it has to be admitted, a rather pessimistic strand of thought manifest here that despairs of humanity responding to the witness of the prophets except by killing them.

The other group singled out in 6.15 are the kings of the earth and the nobles and commanders. Here there is a reaction of fear, though as 9.20 and 11.10 indicate, this does not mean repentance. Here and in 18.9ff. those who have most to lose in the present order of things are mentioned. Of course, others are beneficiaries of that unjust system. Even slaves may consider that they have much to lose if their own masters lose control. On the basis of the maxim 'better the devil you know', many of those now exploited would prefer to hang on to the little that they have rather than risk change. They too will be among those who worship the Beast (13.16). The dominant ideology, that the way things are is 'natural' or 'ordered by God', pervades human consciousness, particularly when it is reinforced by the propaganda of those who wield political and economic power. The kings of the earth and the nobles think that their exercise of power demonstrates their fitness to rule. Revelation shows things differently. It demonstrates the fragility of life which may seem secure and the ease with which the power of the mighty can evaporate. It also contrasts those who fear disastrous change with those who fear God in their lives. The vision of them is what appears next; they are the ones who are truly fit to be rulers of the earth (20.4).

Deliverance for the people of God
7

This chapter appears at first sight to be out of place, offering like ch. 14 a fulfilment of the eschatological hope. Some have seen this as an example of a later addition. This is unlikely because the chapter fits reasonably naturally into the sequence of the apocalypse. It picks up a theme of chs. 5–6, sealing, and relates that issue to the body of the elect. The opening of the seals had unleashed the Four Horsemen with their destructive potential. The catalogue of destruction is suddenly interrupted in ch. 7. The opening of the seals of the book prompts another image : the sealing of the servants of God with the seal (mark) of the living God (cf. Ezek. 9.4). The procession of the redeemed is a true Israel (7.4) which extends to include a multitude from all nations (7.9) who look for the victory of God's justice when 'never again shall they feel hunger or thirst ... and God will wipe away every tear from their eyes' (7.16f.). There is a contrast here similar to that found in chs. 13 and 14. There the contrast is between bearing the mark of the Beast (13.17; 14.9) and having the name of God written on the forehead (14.1). Here the opening of the seals means judgement for a disobedient world, whereas there is hope for those who are sealed with God's name.

The elect are in one sense in a privileged position as they are not harmed by the terrible insects which afflict the world (9.4). That does not mean that they are free from harm, however. As other passages of Revelation indicate (6.9; 11.1ff.; 14.11) the protection from the wrath of God does not guarantee either the spiritual or physical well-being of God's servants. They are always under pressure to conform (chs. 2–3; 13). Those who stand up for the ways of God will find themselves at the receiving end of the anger and retribution of the rich and powerful, who will see their death as a reason for rejoicing because that which pricks their conscience has been removed from the scene (11.10).

John is asked about the identity of the multitude by one of the elders, but is not able to answer. He is told that they are survivors of (in that they have not succumbed to) the great tribulation. 'They are those who have passed through the great ordeal; they have washed their robes and made them white in the blood of the Lamb' (7.14). Once again we have an example of that harsh juxtaposition of ideas: making robes white in blood. We do not need to be too precise about what is meant. The vision here, like passages in Paul's letters (e.g. II Cor. 4.10 and Col. 1.24) express that conviction that Jesus continues to be crucified in the injustices of our fallen world. Here as elsewhere (1.5; 5.10) the eschatological role of the multitude involves an extension of the priestly ministry to the whole of God's people. There is a curious reversal of roles in 7.17. It is not a shepherd who guides the sheep, but one of the flock, a Lamb, albeit one who shares the throne of God.

There is a fulfilment of the promise of Jesus in the Beatitudes (Luke 6.20ff., cf. Isa. 49.10). The promise fulfilled in 7.16 suggests that the blessed are particularly those who have suffered hunger and thirst in the present age (*never again* shall they feel hunger and thirst). The promise is focussed on the needy and outcast, therefore, rather than confined to all those who profess the name of Christ. As we shall see, such confession must involve a pattern of activity in society to justify the presence of one's name in the Lamb's book of life (13.8). The focus on the needy and the least significant is what we should expect from the letters to the seven churches. It is the outwardly least prosperous and famous churches (Smyrna and Philadelphia) which are singled out for commendation and support by the Risen Christ, whereas the distinguished and outwardly spiritual are shown to be dead or lukewarm (Sardis and Laodicea). That uncomfortable message is one we do well to ponder when we react negatively to the suggestion that there should be a preferential option for the poor. We may respond by asserting the universality of God's love and of human sinfulness. Difference of social situation and status demands a different response, however. We cannot take refuge in the fallenness of humanity to presume upon God to ignore the demand of repentance. For the rich and those integrated into society there is much greater temptation to be lukewarm and to offer support, however tacit, for the Beast and Babylon. The poor and the marginalized usually have nothing to gain from such a course of action.

A stark contrast is offered between the way of God and the way of unjust world order. Sealing means recognition by God and hope for the former; opening of seals means judgement for the latter. We learn from Rev. 13 that the true servants of God are those who refuse to succumb to the worship of the Beast. In this they are followers of the one on whom God the Father has set his seal (John 6.27). The graciousness of God to those who follow the Lamb is tenderly brought out in 7.16. It is a passage like this which injects a theme which seems to be lacking elsewhere in Revelation. There is so much talk of divine wrath and human intiative to do the works acceptable to God that the divine grace which enables salvation and holiness to become a reality seem almost totally absent. We appear to be left in an awkward period waiting for ultimate redemption but with scarce resources and mounting obstacles to our achieving our goal. Much of Revelation seems to be devoid of tenderness and present comfort. That is both realistic in its challenge and yet we also miss the hints of God's activity sustaining and enabling that continued witness to Christ in the present. God's grace *is* comforting – but for the task of being truly human. That cannot mean idolatrous behaviour, follow-ing the Beast or being dazzled by Babylon. Those who really reflect God's will may seem foolish. Their path will almost certainly not be easy.

The ones who are sealed are of the tribes of Israel, beginning with the tribe of Judah from which the Messiah comes (5.5). John's vision seems to countenance, like Rom. 11.25, the incorporation of Israel into the new age. It is probably the Gentile remnant that is referred to in 7.9. As in 14.1 they stand in a mood of festivity reminiscent of the Feast of Tabernacles (cf. Lev. 23.40ff. and Ps. 118.25). In the midst of death and destruction a glimpse is offered of those who have with integrity refused to accept injustice and been willing to pay the price for it. In many parts of the world there have been those who have refused to go along with prevailing culture and held out for something better which encompasses the welfare of all men and women, indeed the whole of creation. Frequently they have had to pay for it with their lives, whether by forfeiting a comfortable existence or life itself. Washing robes and making them white in the blood of the Lamb is no specifically 'churchy' affair, therefore. It is not here a matter of being orthodox in belief or devoted in religious practice, but identifying with the Lamb. The mark of identification is a life like his. Whether that involves explicit church involvement or not we are only left to guess. That appears to be of secondary importance, however, to the fundamentally important task of not conforming to the negative aspects of the prevailing culture and holding on to a way of life that is different. Doing this is nothing less than identification with the way of Jesus, which for him ended up in the brutal death on the cross: 'Jesus continues to be crucified in all those who are crucified in history ... in the millions who go hungry every day.'[1]

[1] Leonardo Boff, *Way of the Cross, Way of Justice*, ET Orbis Books 1980, p. 92.

The natural world becomes a series of nightmares
8–9

Many of the points made in connection with the threefold sequence have already been discussed under ch. 6 and need not be repeated here. What we find in the inexorable sequence of seals and trumpets is a move into a world that is even more nightmarish. This word is used advisedly. Our horrid dreams, however much dread they cause us and however much we prefer not to recall them, are substantial comments on us and our society. John's 'nightmare' is the reality of judgement. The fantastic and horrifying description of the torments which await those who are not sealed (9.4) brings to the surface our deepest fears about our destruction. They evoke primitive fears of poisonous and dangerous insects, the disruption of the natural world so that it becomes a threat rather than a part of our existence. Our generation can perhaps appreciate something of that fear if only it will allow itself to do so. The threat to the environment is one that is often talked about. The problem is that we like our way of life and are unwilling to do much more than tinker with a response. When we decide to respond, it will probably be too late.

Apparently John offers a hope of the elect escaping the torment of judgement (9.4, cf. 7.3). References elsewhere in Revelation should warn us that it is no part of the message of Revelation to suggest that God's servants will escape. The fate of Antipas (2.13) and that of the two witnesses (11.7f.) indicate that there is no miraculous escape from the horrors of suffering and tribulation (unlike the stories in Daniel 3 and 6). Those who suggest that there is to be some miraculous rescue by a divine rapture to heaven *before suffering* ignore the clear expectation that there is a task of prophetic witness and service to be done. The judgement on Jerusalem prophesied by Ezekiel in Ezek. 9.1ff. involved the marking with a cross on the forehead those 'who groan and lament over all the abominations practised here' (9.4). That does not mean any easy life for God's prophet (as the careers of Ezekiel and Jeremiah indicate), or any distance from the judgement which is to come (something Jesus recognizes too in Mark 13.14ff.).

The worst fears surface in the gruesome catalogue that issues forth from the trumpet blasts. Insects take on human and animal form (9.8ff.). Locusts were a plague to humanity, and the sting of the scorpion is proverbially threatening. Yet the creatures are girded with weapons of war (9.9), and the threat of the angelic host who are bound at the Euphrates (9.14) is military in its depiction. John's vision is of the awefulness and destructive potential of war. Creatures which are not frightening in themselves become thus in John's vision. The full destructive power of nature is set loose as it is transformed into something far more threatening than the occasional plague of locusts or the poisonous sting. The angel of the abyss is at their head (9.11). It is from the abyss that the Beast comes (11.7, cf. 13.1 and 17.11). In nature and in society the destructive power consequent on rebellion against God the Creator is everywhere to be seen. The angels are loosed in v. 14 just as Satan is loosed to bring about the last battle at Armageddon (20.7). Only the binding of Satan allows the messianic age. This suggests that the consequence of the rejection of the coming of the Messiah leads to the release of a power which might have been differently and more creatively channelled if it had been devoted to God and the Messiah.

The opening of the seventh seal brings about silence in heaven. The seeming inevitability of this process is interrupted, and the pause enables reflection on the awesome and terrible character of what is happening, even in heaven. Silence and reflection are appropriate in the midst of the tumult and catastrophe of life (Ps. 46; Zech. 2.13). At the decisive council in Acts 15 a reaction of silence greets the stories that are told and is a prelude to the awesome decisions that are taken (15.12). Silence is an appropriate response in the light of this coming of God in wrath. Gustavo Gutierrez reminds us:

In our dealings with the poor we encounter the Lord (see Matthew 25.31–46), but this encounter in turn makes our solidarity with the poor more radical and more authentic. Contemplation and commitment within history are fundamental dimensions of Christian practice ... The mystery reveals itself through prayer and solidarity with the poor. I call Christian life the 'first act'; only then can this life inspire a process of reflection, which is the 'second act'.

Contemplation and commitment combine to form what may be called the phase of *silence* before God. . . . Silence is a condition for any loving encounter with God in prayer and commitment . . . Theology is talk that is constantly enriched by silence.[1]

The sounding ot the trumpet marks the messianic age and warns of the need for penitence in the face of judgement. The trumpet blasts announce the great and terrible day of the Lord (cf. I Cor. 15.26; Joel 2.1; I Thess. 4.15f.).[2] Before the trumpets begin to sound there is the offering of prayers of the saints at the heavenly altar. There is a potent reminder of the *effectiveness* of the human activity of prayer and witness. Prayers *do* 'get further than the ceiling'; apparently futile witness is noticed in heaven. For people who thought it did not matter whether they prayed, how they behaved or whether they stood up to be counted, the thunder and lightning in 8.5, reminiscent of the theophany in 4.5 (cf. Ex. 19.6 and Isa. 29.6), emphasize the significance of the prayers in the divine economy. The ascent of the smoke contrasts with the smoke that comes up from the abyss in 9.1 and the smoke of the torment of the followers of the Beast in 14.11. The smoke of the incense, the prayers of the saints, ascends to God. It is an acceptable offering, not a threat to the world (unlike the smoke in 9.1). Of course, the prayers stand as a reproach to the injustice and lack of repentance.

Humanity longs for release (9.6) but does not find it. Cain killed his brother and his penalty was not to be killed but to be marked (as are those who worship the Beast – 13.16 and 14.11). It is as if humanity is brought face to face with the full horror of the world it has created. The ultimate idolatry is to make the creature the goal and measure of creation. That leads to darkness (9.2), disfigurement and the un-balancing of the natural world. The death and destruction that has taken place up to this point constitutes the first woe. We are told that there are two more woes to come (9.12). Three woes are cried over the inhabitants of the earth in 8.13. Only one further woe is mentioned in 11.14. The absence of any mention of the third woe may be an indication that the final consummation is still awaited. We as readers have a drama before us which is partly complete and we are (as it were) offered a preview of the ending. We stand in the midst of the trials and tribulations awaiting their climax. All that can be

---

[1] Gustavo Gutierrez, *The Truth Shall Make You Free*, ET Orbis Books 1990, p. 3.
[2] See also Ivor Jones, *Music. A Joy for Ever*, Epworth 1989, pp. 43f.

done is watch, wait, witness and not be led astray (cf. Mark 13.9, 33ff.).

Still the injustice persists (9.20f.): 'The rest of humanity who survived these plagues still did not renounce the gods their hands had made or cease the worship of demons and of idols fashioned from gold, silver, bronze, stone and wood, which cannot see or hear or walk; nor did they repent of their murders, their sorcery, their fornication or their robberies.'

We are offered a picture of life going on as before with no sense on humanity's part that anything is amiss with the way in which they are conducting themselves. Instead, as 16.21 indicates, the dwellers on earth blame God for the dislocation of life (note the allusion to Ps. 115.4f., where the contrast is offered between 'our God' and 'their idols'). This will manifest itself in particular political institutions in a subsequent vision. It is not surprising, therefore, that idolatry is identified as the fundamental problem. It will be accompanied by evil deeds which exhibit disorder. We shall be shown the ultimate demonstration of murder, idolatry and robbery in the form of Babylon and its cruel regime (chs. 17–18). Its sorcery is the use and maintenance of power without reference to God. Revelation pauses in the midst of the final sequence of plagues to comment on the inability of humanity to understand and repent (16.9, 11, 21, cf. Mark 4.11–12).

The death and vindication of the two prophetic witnesses
10–11

There is an interruption in the sequence of trumpet blasts after 9.22 where the imperviousness of humanity to the disordered world around them is stressed. As we have seen, there is a long interlude (punctuated by the seventh trumpet blast in 11.13) in which visions concerning the church, its role, its fate and the threat to it are touched on.

A mysterious angel now appears at a crucial juncture in the unfolding story immediately after the refusal of humanity to repent. This angel has characteristics reminiscent of Christ (1.16) and God (4.3). The angel possesses an open scroll ready to read, parallel with the closed scroll in ch. 5. The angel's proclamation is a serious one and has all the marks of God's presence. Whereas John's prophecy is written and left unsealed, what the seven thunders say is not allowed to be written down, but is sealed. The links here with Daniel (cf. Dan. 8.26; 12.4,9) and Ezekiel (Ezek. 2.9) are apparent. The instruction suggests a mysterious character to the noise of the seven thunders, but they cannot match the significance of John's words which are to be written. The angel at last speaks and swears an oath by the Creator. Once again we are to accept the seriousness of the proclamation, the content of which is that there will be no more delay (so rightly REB), rather than no more time (10.6 cf. Hab. 2.3). John uses the word *chronos* here, whereas he often uses *kairos*. It is unlikely that the message proclaims an end of time. That would have been most unusual for one brought up in the Jewish tradition. The coming of the new age did not mean the end of time as such. We are offered a further explanation of what is meant in vv. 7f. The blowing of the seventh trumpet will herald the completion of the mystery of God proclaimed by the prophets. The angelic proclamation, therefore, concerns the imminence of the termination of the time of the present age (cf. IV Ezra 4.50) and the moment when God will demonstrate sovereignty over human affairs (11.17). The process of judgement (like the forbearance of God, cf. Rom. 3.25) is not interminable. That word of reassurance is offered after the horrendous times heralded by the heavenly trumpet blasts. 'If the Lord had not cut short that time of troubles, no living thing could survive' (Mark 13.20). It is a reminder that the message of Revelation is directed to readers at the time to challenge them and is not sealed up merely for generations far ahead (cf. Dan. 12.4).

There follows in ch. 11 a remarkable vision of a besieged temple and two witnesses who stand prophesying for a limited period before their deaths at the hands of the Beast from the abyss. They are vindicated and retaken to heaven, and the earth suffers an earthquake which causes its inhabitants great fear. Ch. 11 ends with the proclamation of the passing of the second woe and the dominion of God. The message of the chapter is relatively clear and its relationship to its immediately preceding context very close. They are linked by the theme of prophecy (10.11, cf. 11.3). The feelings of threat and external pressure from enemies come to the fore, though they lurked as a real problem throughout the letters to the churches. Now the interface between witness and the encroaching world is tackled head on.

According to chs. 10–11, the seer is involved in the unfolding eschatological drama of the apocalypse when he is instructed to eat the scroll and commanded to prophesy. Hitherto he has had a dialogue with the angel (7.13f.) and wept at what he has seen (5.4). Here, as in 1.19, there is a direct commission to act. Here there is a direct call to participate actively as a prophet rather than merely be a passive spectator (10.11). The eating of the scroll is reminiscent of a similar prophetic call in Ezek. 2.9ff. It is a commission which comes in a context of much urgency (10 6). Like the Lamb in ch. 5, the prophet of the Lamb takes the scroll. The scroll mentioned in 5.1 reappears in 10.2, 8–10 (though it is described as *biblaridion* rather than *biblion* as in 5.1). There are other links between the two passages, e.g. the reference to a mighty angel in 5.2 and 10.1f. Just as the Lamb received the scroll from God, so now John (and the prophetic community) are given a central role in continuing the Lamb's witness before the world. The universal sovereignty of the Lamb (5.9) is reflected in the universal scope of the message of the prophet (10.11). The message is internalized (10.9) and forms part of the very being of the prophet. Prophecy is no longer merely an uttering of oracles but involves the whole of life. That is what was wrong with Balaam's prophecy. He uttered the words of God, but his life was not what God expected (cf. 2.14). In ch. 11 the prophetic role encompasses every aspect of life (and death). That was something experienced by all true prophets of God (Luke 11.49), particularly Jeremiah, whose call is evoked in 10.11 (cf. Jer. 1.10). Prophets could expect a life of witness, suffering and death, so that wherever they live or die would be a repetition of what their Lord suffered (11.8). The holy city which according to 11.2 is profaned is also a place of profanity on the same level as Sodom and Gomorrah. It is a telling reminder that there is no unambiguously holy place. That will apply to churches and holy places anywhere. They are all sites of human conflict and the possible profanation of God's word.

Utilizing the ideas connected in the Old Testament with the figures of Moses and Elijah (11.6, cf. Ex. 7–11 and I Kings 17) the prophetic witness takes place in a social setting opposed to God. That witness must take place even though it ends up with martyrdom in death. The history of the interpretation of this passage makes fascinating reading. Suggestions about the identity of the two witnesses (11.3) range from Peter and Paul to Enoch and Elijah. In ancient Christian commentaries it was supposed that they represent an eschatological witness which would happen, Elijah-like, before the great and terrible day of the Lord (cf. Malachi 4.5). The juxtaposition of the command to John to prophesy in 10.11 and the following vision makes it more likely that we are offered an exemplification of true prophecy, its effects and its cost.

Revelation is insistent that the role of the martyr or witness is of central importance. Jesus of Nazareth is the faithful prophetic witness, and his followers have to continue that testimony of Jesus. That will involve suffering in the great tribulation. The prophetic commission is followed, in ch. 11, by a vision in which the church is offered a paradigm of the true prophetic witness as it sets out to fulfil its vocation to prophesy before the world. The measuring of the temple symbolizes the present, limited extent of the divine possession in a world where the rebellious nations are in apparent control (11.2). It is as if temporarily God has only a precarious foothold in the world. The act of measuring occurs again in 21.15 where the angelic companion of John is about to measure the new Jerusalem, and John offers an inventory of its contents (22.16ff.). In that passage the whole of the city belongs to God as in the vision of the new city in Ezek. 40. 3ff. In ch. 11 there is a temple and an altar (these have already been mentioned, but they are in *heaven* rather than on earth – 7.15; 8.3; 15.5; 11.19; 6.9). Here these are measured and the rest is left. In the new Jerusalem *everything* is measured; there, everything unambiguously belongs to God and is holy. Here, although God is in reality Creator and sovereign Lord, the nations of the world are in temporary control (cf. Luke 21.24). The area which is left to God is focussed on the community of those who gather to worship and on earth mirror the praise of heaven where God is acknowledged as Creator and sovereign (4.11). So God is not left without witness (11.3ff.). The proximity of those opposed to God and to the faithful community (v. 2) is apparent throughout Revelation. Some of the communities have experienced what happens to faithful witnesses already (2.13, cf. 11.7f.) and can expect that mix of explicit threat and constant pressure to conform characteristic of an unjust social order.

The plagues with which the two witnesses are able to strike the earth remind us of chs. 6, 8–9 and 16 (especially 16.4). The prophets have the power to bind and loose (cf. Matt. 16.19; Rev. 20.1f.). Their actions torment humanity in the way that the plagues of the eschatological judgement of God do (cf. 16.10). The life of prophets is not one of niceness and respectability, therefore. They are expected to torment. But that feeling of torment is one that is felt by those who cannot cope with God's justice and prefer not to acknowledge it. It is the torment of the prick of conscience and the dim realization that what is normally seen as acceptable may not in fact be so.

For the first time we have the mention of the Beast in 11.7. It comes from the abyss whose smoke had darkened creation and had produced the plague of locusts (9.3f.). The keeping in check of those dark and destructive forces by God (cf. Ps. 104.9, where God fixes the waters of chaos so that they may no longer threaten the earth; cf. Rev 9.14) has enabled a *semblance* of order, but that period of order has been abused and the coming of the Messiah means an end to the *illusion* of order and the manifestation of the full extent of *dis*order and suffering. The time has come when God would take the power and reign (11.15 and 17f.). The activity of the Beast is to make war on the witnesses (cf. 17.14; 13.7; 16.14; 19.19). The destructive potential of the Beast is, however, limited because (as we shall soon see) its power has been defeated (12.7). Vindication is assured (11.11). Just as every eye will see the central importance of the crucified Messiah (1.7), so also will the enemies of God's witnesses (11.12). The mention of the Beast here indicates that the prophecy is no hole and corner affair but attracts the attention of political power and its antagonism (so 10.11; cf. Mark 13.9).

The lack of concern for human dignity is evident in the refusal to bury the bodies of the prophets (11.8) and the profanity of the rejoicing over their deaths. Such lack of concern for human rights is symptomatic of a world which turns its back on God's justice. The inhabitants of the world are under the misapprehension that the removal of God's witnesses will mean an end to torment. Beliefs of that kind are commonplace. The opponents of human rights of the poor in El Salvador thought that the assassination of Archbishop Oscar Romero in 1980 would rid them of the torment of one who continued to remind them of injustice. God's purposes are never thwarted in this way. As Romero himself said, two weeks before his assassination:

> I have frequently been threatened with death. I ought to say that, as a Christian, I do not believe in death without resurrection. If they kill me I will rise again in the people of El Salvador. I am not boasting, I say it with the greatest humility. I am bound, as a pastor, by a divine command to give my life for those whom I love, and that is all Salvadoreans, even those who are going to kill me. If they manage to carry out their threats, from this moment I offer my blood for the redemption and resurrection of El Salvador. Martyrdom is a grace from God which I do not believe I deserve. But if God accepts the sacrifice of my life, then may my blood be the seed of liberty, and a sign of hope that will soon become a reality. May my death, if it is accepted by God, be for the liberation of my people, and as a witness of hope in what is to come. Can you tell them, if they succeed in killing me, that I pardon and bless those who do it? But I wish that they could realize that they are wasting their time. A bishop may die, but the church of God, which is the people, will never die.[1]

---

[1] From J. Sobrino, *Romero: Martyr for Liberation*, Catholic Institute for International Relations 1982, p. 76.

The dragon pursues his quarry

12

Juxtaposed with the vision of the two witnesses, their death and vindication is another vision about persecution. The message is once again quite a simple one: a pregnant woman is threatened by a dragon. She gives birth to a male child who is precious to God as the Messiah (12.5, cf. Ps. 2.9). There is divine protection for both. In the case of the woman, it is the wilderness, a particular place of importance for God's people (Ex. 15.22ff.; Hosea 2.14; Mark 1.3ff.). Although the woman was taken to be a reference to the Virgin Mary in later Christian tradition, it is probably preferable to take it as a way of referring to the people of God from whom the Messiah is born and whose members are persecuted by those forces opposed to God. The identity of the woman is made clear in v. 17. We are told that the dragon made war with the rest of her offspring . These are those who keep the commands of God and hold to the testimony of Jesus. There is a close link between the male child and the rest of her seed, suggesting the kind of link between the Messiah as a child of Abraham and all those who have faith in the Messiah which Paul expounds in Gal. 3–4. This is not a right but rooted in particular types of behaviour (12.17, cf. Matt. 3.7ff. and I John 4.10).

John's vision of the woman owes something to Old Testament dreams such as Gen. 37.9. There is also a contrast with the vision of Babylon in ch. 17. In ch. 12 a place is provided for the woman in the wilderness, a place where the people of God were formed and nurtured (cf. Hosea 2.14). Similarly in ch. 17 John is taken off to the wilderness to behold Babylon seated on the seven-headed, ten-horned Beast (17.3). These characteristics mark the dragon (12.3) which persecutes the woman surrounded by the sun. As in the picture of the woman in ch. 17, the woman in ch. 12 is passive. She is a victim. Babylon is supported by the Beast and is subject to the vagaries of the Beast's behaviour; the woman here is pursued by the Dragon and is dependent on God. That kind of portrayal does offend our activist outlook on life in which we prefer pictures of women to conform to 'male' stereotypes of power, responsibility, autonomy and involvement. The picture offered of Jesus in the closing chapters of the gospels is of a victim. To wait and to watch is a vocation which our age finds so difficult and may be all that is possible, practicable in order to maintain integrity and compassion.

A constant theme in the chapter revolves around the contrast between heaven and earth. We are offered contrasts between two signs: the woman clothed in the sun and the fiery dragon, triumph in heaven for the agents of God and the threat to earth. Nowhere is that contrast more clearly seen than in the consequence of the war in heaven which results in the dragon/Satan being thrown down. That guarantees God's kingdom (12.10) and the freedom of the 'brethren' from prosecution in the divine court (12.10, cf. Rom. 8.37). The dragon is here depicted in the Old Testament guise of Satan the accuser (Job 1.9–11; Zech. 3.1). Paul was to put the issue in slightly different terms, though, interestingly enough, drawing on the language of a law court. He talked of believers being justified and of there being no condemnation for those in Christ Jesus (Rom. 8.1). The reason for this is that there is no longer a prosecuting counsel in the heavenly court, only a defending counsel, Jesus Christ 'who makes intercession for us' (Rom. 8.33f., especially v. 34; Christ 'pleads our cause', cf. I John 2.1).

The throwing down of Satan (12.9) is a theme hinted at elsewhere in the New Testament as the moment of eschatological triumph (Luke 10.18; John 12.31). It is a sign that disorder is at an end (in Luke it appears after the disciples return reporting their triumph over the powers of darkness) and restoration is taking place. Here the ejection of Satan from heaven is not linked with the death of Christ, though elsewhere the cross is seen as the moment of the triumph over the powers (e.g. I Cor. 2.9; I Peter 3.20).[1] It is important that we do not assume that triumph in the heavenly battle is focussed solely on the cross. More important is the juxtaposition of the war in heaven and the birth of the male child who is clearly the Messiah (12.5, cf. Ps. 2.9) and like the Lamb, the Lion of Judah, snatched up to God's throne (5.5). The two signs in heaven should be taken as the clues to interpret the chapter : the woman is persecuted and bears a child; the

[1] See further G.B. Caird, *Principalities and Powers. A Study in Pauline Theology*, Clarendon Press 1956, and Walter Wink, *Naming the Powers: the Language of Power in the New Testament*, Fortress 1984, and *Unmasking the Powers: the Invisible Forces that Determine Human Existence*, Fortress 1986.

dragon persecutes and is thrown out of heaven. The last-mentioned event takes place immediately after the birth and nurture of the male child is mentioned, suggesting that the arrival of the messianic age coincides with the ejection of Satan from heaven. That is exactly what we would expect from passages like Luke 10.18 and John 12.31.

The snatching to God is paralleled elsewhere in the New Testament. The same verb is used of ascents to heaven. In II Cor. 12.2ff. Paul talks about being snatched up to Paradise. In I Thess. 4.17 the elect are caught up to meet Christ at the Parousia. In Wisdom of Solomon 4.10 the mysterious disappearance of Enoch, hinted at in Gen. 5.24, is described in similar terms. Here in Rev. 12.5 the Messiah is snatched up to God and the throne of God. This pattern of rapture raises the possibility of its applicability to the much discussed passage in Phil. 2.6, where it is said of Christ that 'he laid no claim to equality with God'. The word translated 'claim to equality' in this verse is related to the verb *harpazo* used in the passages mentioned. Possibly in Phil. 2.5 (where RSV translates 'did not count equality with God a thing to be grasped') Paul has in mind the divine snatching up to heaven such as is spoken of in Rev. 12.5 and paralleled in the story of Elijah's ascent in II Kings 2. The point would be then that for Jesus there was no divine rapture which would bring about salvation and so avoid the pain of death. Rather he emptied himself and was obedient and accepting of death. It was *that* which was the basis for the defeat of the powers (Phil. 2.10f.) and his exaltation. Precisely that point is implied in the triumph of the Lamb with the marks of slaughter in Rev. 5, and the presentation of the glorification of Jesus according to the Gospel of John, which comes via the cross. Vindication and triumph are earned by the Messiah, not seen as a matter of right. The same is true for his followers (Rev. 7.14; 12.17).

The bringing to birth of the messianic age and its alternative value-system is a threat to those who would keep this age in being (called Satan or the dragon in Rev. 12 and 'the god of this age' in II Cor. 4.4). This elaborate mythology is very down to earth in the sense that it represents a clear warning of the tangibility of the threat (12.12) and the superhuman significance of the struggle going on. The heavenly struggle is closely linked with the earthly struggle of those who seek to be disciples of Jesus in maintaining their testimony (12.10). The maintenance of that in the face of temptations to compromise is the equivalent in the realm of flesh and blood of the overcoming of the forces of darkness in heaven by Michael and the angels of light. Here the imagery of apocalyptic reminds us that in ordinary activity we are engaged in a struggle which is no ordinary matter. The war in heaven is extended to earth. The defeated Satan conducts a campaign with threats, bribes, deception and social and economic ostracism (see ch. 13 especially 13.16). It is a war waged against the woman's seed, the target the prevention of obedience to God's commands and the witness to Jesus (12.17). Why? These are the essence of activity in obedience to the Messiah. The letter to the Ephesians coincides with Rev. 12 in stressing the extraordinary character of the struggle that Christians are engaged in (Eph. 6.10). That is an inevitable continuation of the privileged role of the people of God, involved as it is in the task of continuing the cosmic struggle begun by Jesus (Eph. 2.5; 3.5; cf. Matt. 16.17). This is not to be seen solely in individual moral struggles. As Rev. 13 makes clear, it is just as much a struggle in the political and economic sphere. That fact has been perceived by our brothers and sisters in South Africa. Here is what Allan Boesak has to say:

> Jesus came, not simply to pour oil on our wounds or cover up the sinfulness of the world. He came to destroy the works of Satan. He did this not by matching the power of Satan with equal power; not with propaganda or violence; nor with the simple, pietistic sentimentality of the sweet, gentle Jesus invented by Western Christianity. He did it by his incarnation, his identification with the poor, the meek, and the lowly; by his engagement in the struggle for God's kingdom of *shalom* and justice and love, even at the price of his life ... To be reconciled means to face the truth about ourselves and about the things we do to each other. It cannot mean covering up the truth because it is too painful. It means confrontation with the evil in the world, the evil within us.[2]

That dimension is also apparent in the story of Jesus. The testing of God's Son by Satan goes on in the activities of human opponents (the same verb is used of the activity of Satan and of the Pharisees and Herodians in Mark 1.11 and 12.15). What is going on in the life of Jesus is no ordinary struggle but involves superhuman forces manifest in human alliances and institutions (cf. Mark 3.22f.). We cannot separate one from the other. Human struggles to keep one's integrity

[2] Allan Boesak, *Comfort and Protest*, pp. 86 and 88.

by keeping the testimony of Jesus are intimately bound up with the whole project of God to bring about the Kingdom of God.

There is little doubt that talk of Satan leaves our generation cold. It seems to represent notions of primitive beliefs or the fantasies of infancy which adults need to grow out of if they are to be mature persons. Thus when John talks about Satan's throne and synagogue we probably find ourselves reacting negatively to such hostility and polarization. The symbolism of evil in the Bible ranks with fairy stories as a problem area for our contemporary world. Bruno Bettelheim has reminded us of the importance of even the most grotesque fairy tales as means of getting in touch with the darker side of ourselves and our relationships.[3] It is no less true of the symbolism of evil. By that I do not mean little devils sitting on roof tops to invade homes, or even preoccupation with individual possession and exorcism but something more subtle and altogether more pervasive.

The most important thing which Revelation helps us come to terms with is that Satan is a symbol of the reality of all that is opposed to our presence with God (12.10). As an accuser Satan's role is one that is not easily defined, and certainly is not to be simplistically identified with embodiments of evil in individuals. Indeed, Revelation makes it very clear that the manifestation of Satan's power is complex, corporate, and institutional. Thus the Beast symbolizes a concrete embodiment of evil power. That is not a single king but an imperial institution or structure, a whole way of ruling with its various human manifestations (13.1ff.) and its agents of propaganda. Likewise Babylon is not an individual but a whole network of human relationships and institutions who contribute to a pattern of life which John can describe as 'fornication'. Revelation refuses to allow us to confine our scope of the embodiment of evil to what we can manage (e.g. the individual) just as it refuses to allow us to confine the horizon of hope and salvation thus. Its symbolism should not lead us to identify what is described solely with an eschatological manifestation of evil. As the writer of I John reminds us, Antichrists are active, especially in places we least expect (I John 2.19). For the author of that epistle it was erstwhile, faithful members of the community who had now separated themselves. I John is a salutary reminder, echoed by Revelation itself, that preoccupation with the Antichrist at the end of time may blind us to the abomination of the Antichrist in our midst.

[3] Bruno Bettelheim, *The Uses of Enchantment. The Meaning and Importance of Fairy Tales*, Penguin 1991.

Revelation refuses to allow us the satisfaction of certainty about the location of Satan's acts. We may be sure that the church is not immune from Satan's activities. Revelation has no truck with the branding of others as satanic without noting the evil in oneself. Evil is not something over there in others, in other countries or in the last days; it is here. The struggle against evil is one that needs to be recognized and identified with as much precision as possible. It is clearly winnable because it is rooted in the triumph of the Lamb. The means of conquest are identification with the Lamb (12.17; 14.12; 15.2). The unmasking of the Beast and Babylon suggests that apparently benign institutions and those involved in supporting them can be exponents of that which is most profoundly opposed to God. It was after all the activity of clerks, drivers and signalmen who through mindless bureaucracy kept the abomination of the Holocaust going just as much as the more notorious camp officials. Revelation makes it quite clear that the system of evil has so many going along with it and giving it support that the language of Satan and demons is perhaps the only way of drawing attention to the extent of its iniquity. The task of understanding the extent of its deception and its flattery is costly but essential. It is entirely consistent with the practice of Jesus who not only rooted out evil in the individual but sought to do so in a society as well, and by his death tore down that symbol of power and mystery which was the means of control of the institution of evil of his day, the temple. What was apparently there to serve God had become barren and demonic. The agent of God's kingdom could not fulfil his role without dealing with its influence, and so he goes up to Jerusalem and meets the resistance of its operators. The system opposes him and crushes him, but in so doing is itself denuded and overcome (Mark 15.38).

Acknowledging and dealing with our feelings of threat

One of the problems posed by Revelation is the uncompromising attitude towards accommodation with the principalities and powers. To many it seems to offer an untenable position, offering only the prospect of patient endurance and suffering rather than the exploration of a healthy compromise. It seems to offer little consolation in the present as we stumble and fall. We must recognize its rigorous message and our need to hear it, for Revelation can contribute to our recognition of our passions within and without. It can also help us come to terms with and assess the threats to ourselves and our world.

There are few individuals who do not suffer feelings of threat, sometimes of an unspecific kind, when confronted by circumstances which trigger feelings of deep insecurity and inability to cope. Most of us have managed in our lives by working out methods of dealing with those situations so that the feelings do not overwhelm us. Lack of recognition of psychological needs leave us bewildered at the ways we feel threatened by persons and situations to a degree which is not entirely appropriate. These deep-seated needs fuel problematic situations and skew our perception of them by magnifying the extent of the threat. All of us need to guarantee a modicum of self-esteem and it is the subconscious recollection of those moments in childhood where our self was lost or left unaffirmed which can contribute to feelings of insecurity and threat in adult life. Adult life may on the whole be a time of the more effective management of our feelings, though the feelings themselves will change little and remain dormant waiting for the opportunity of real vulnerability to pierce the surface of our well-honed protective armour. Dealing with that individual or group insecurity by bluster or defensiveness resists the sharp stab to our vulnerable inner self but at the cost of provoking aggression or distance in relationships. It all masks that real inner self which is so needy (the reality of the wretched, poor, blind, and naked self described in Rev. 3.17). Nakedness is a demeaning and unprotected situation when there appears to be no defence. The manifestation of the totality of our physical selves threatens the opening up of those carefully protected parts of our inner selves which are kept from public view. The judgement of Babylon involves nakedness (cf. 17.16) in which the pretence of the trappings of ill-gotten gain and the insecurity of status are stripped away. We long for protection for that vulnerable, needy and yet so demanding self. Yet the way to fulfil its needs is not by the tactic of the construction of yet more sound defences but the acknowledgement of that need (cf. 2.9) and the nourishment which comes through nourishing our humanity and integrity.

Revelation as a book rubs our noses in the need for honesty about ourselves and our world. The letters to the churches, as we have seen, refuse to allow Christians any false sense of security while affirming very clearly the positive parts of their witness. There is an unmasking of the 'true self' of the life of the community. This should encourage us to explore the extent of our poverty and not suppose, complacently, that we are rich and secure when we need the refining fire of self-knowledge and transformation in the light of the presence of Christ. Thus the reality of our shame and nakedness needs to be exposed (3.18) in accord with the truth.

Feelings of threat and insecurity lie at the heart of the dramatic signs in Rev. 12.[3] They bring us to the heart of the reparation we need in ourselves and our world. The twin visions exhibit negative and positive messages, both of which we should heed. First of all, there is the picture of the woman clothed with the sun. It is in itself a picture of glory. Yet at the same time there is more than a hint of vulnerability and of hope. She is pregnant (12.2) and about to give birth, not a situation in which one can think of defending oneself. Instead she is tormented (sharing the pain of the torment of creation as it experiences God's wrath –the same verb is used of the judge-ment of recalcitrant humanity in 14.11 and 20.10). In that situation she is confronted by the terrible dragon which seeks to devour her offspring. Her hope is about to be cut off at the moment of greatest vulnerability. In that situation she gives birth; her offspring is preserved (12.5) and the woman is cared for (12.6).

Alongside this great sign there is the account of the war in heaven in which the dragon is defeated and thrown down to earth. We are left with the impression that, however great the continuing threat may be from the dragon (12.12), that threat is temporary and ultimately able to be overcome. How is the threat overcome? Rev. 12 suggests two ways: recognition of vulnerability and trust in God; lack of defensiveness and obedience to God and holding the witness of Jesus. There is thus an issue about true and false senses of security. Revelation's advice to its readers is not a defensiveness based on weapons of war or protection of oneself, but the commands of God and the testimony of Jesus (12.17). That will not guarantee that there will be no threat. Rather the *reality* of the threat is as nothing compared with the nakedness that is exposed at the judge-ment of Christ and the impoverishment that one does to oneself by the apparently sensible strategy of self-protection through wealth, property and accommodation with the Beast.

The first glimpse of the woman in the vision as glorious is a reminder of the value and worth of each human and the world in

---

[3] Rev. 12 is a chapter treated at length by C.G. Jung in his *Answer to Job*, ch. 13 (Ark Paperbacks 1984, pp. 120ff.; in *Psychology and Religion*, Collected Works XI, Routledge and Kegan Paul 1969[2], pp. 126ff.).

which they live (John 3.16). True security is rooted in that fact: man and woman created in God's image and likeness (Gen. 1.26f.). The woman is glorious yet vulnerable. Her security rests solely in God. It is that theme which runs through Isa. 40ff. (indeed note the link between Isa. 49.6, 10 and Rev. 7.6, 16f.). Those chapters, like Revelation, open our eyes to the greatness of God's purposes in a situation where God the Creator seems as nothing compared with the might of the nations and their gods. The futility of the false sense of security in idolatry and the role and importance of the apparently insignificant are stressed. In Isa. 40 God comforts Israel and reminds them of the inscrutability of the divine purposes and the perspective of the Creator as compared with the creature. In Isa. 42 we see that there is a task for a weak, impoverished human in bringing forth justice for the nations. In Isa. 43 there is a reminder of the intensity of God's love for the people. They are special and known intimately and personally: 'Have no fear, for I have redeemed you; I call you by name, you are mine. When you pass through water I shall be with you; when you pass through rivers they will not overwhelm you ...' (Isa. 43.1f.). That knowledge and affection are themes hinted at in Rev. 3.9 (cf. Isa. 43.4; 49.23), and the divine support for the vulnerable is the resource for the safety of the woman (12.14, cf. Isa. 40.31).

It is that which is the basis for real security and worth, for there is no human nurture which can ultimately be relied upon, nor any defensive strategy which will ultimately protect. To be secure in oneself is to be secure in God and to accept oneself as worthy and glorious in the sight of God; to know we may not always be able to *feel* it. That is no easy task, but is the root of a sense of worth which does not have to rely on the ephemeral nature of false gods. Idols are our own creation and, as John reminds us, ultimately involve us in the worship of Satan, the very one whose threat we long to escape from. That false sense of ourselves superficially seems to protect and yet in fact is *untrue* to who we really are and what we really need. That was grasped in different ways in prayers of Thomas Cranmer. His words 'to whom all hearts are open, all desires known and from no secrets are hid' are truly in the spirit of Revelation. It reminds us that the one with whom we have to deal searches the very depths of our being (2.23), and there is no point in masking the reality by resort to appearances or those defences we have used to construct space for ourselves.

A disturbing aspect of the vision of the woman and the dragon, however, is the way in which nurture and protection turns out to be such a risky business. There seems to be no guarantee that there will be any assistance as the ruthless pursuit by the dragon continues. One feature of this vision which can be missed is the parallel between the woman in Rev. 12 and Hagar, who finds relief in the wilderness after being ill-treated by Sarah (Gen.16.6) and ejected by Abraham (Gen. 21.14). That sense of being special and then being rejected by the group which seems to have God on its side is one that many share. Indeed, it may well have formed part of the early Christian experience of bewilderment as they found themselves rejected by non-Christian Jews with whom they had so much in common. Even in that situation of exclusion and apparent God-forsakenness there is succour for Hagar (Gen. 16.7; 21.19).

All this is of equal relevance to our social world. Here the individual, group or nation constructs defences to ward off threats to its insecurities. It resorts to its rights. Nowhere is this more obviously seen than in the way property is used to guarantee our security and our value. The concept of private property is foreign to the Bible. After all, 'the earth is the Lord's' (Ps. 24.1; Lev. 25.23). Security is not rooted in the gaining and protecting of space but in God and God's love. It matters not in Rev. 11 that the courts of the temple are trampled by the nations provided that there are those who maintain God's vision in their lives. We need a sense of worth, but that can never be rooted in space kept exclusively for ourselves as our private property or in the status we gain. For that reason, if no other, the pursuit of wealth is futile, and those who have engaged in that activity are are frequently shown in Revelation to be victims of a delusion. Living in community as God's people involves sharing a city and a garden (chs. 21–2) but above all being aware of one's worth (the elect are stamped with the name of God and see God's face equally – 22.4). There there will be no intrusion on one another because there will be no need to preserve space for oneself to secure a sense of self-esteem. The understanding of oneself as worthy in the sight of God demands the maintenance of an identity not by resort to the strategies of this age but with the perspective of faithfulness and witness to the one who embodies the image of the invisible God (cf. Col. 1.15).

The apparent triumph of evil
13

The consequence of the defeat of Satan is that no place is found in heaven (12.8), and so he is is thrown down to earth (12.9). The earth is now the arena of Satan's activities (12.12) and a particular target of his attack is 'those who keep God's commandments and maintain their witness to Jesus' (12.17). We are then shown the particular manifestation of that activity: the self-satisfied institution bent on its own glorification. The passage picks up on the tradition of representing nations by beasts found in Dan. 7, thus indicating the political character of that chapter and the way references to it should be read in the rest of the New Testament. The political symbolism is very much to the fore in the second half of Revelation. In comparison with Daniel here only one Beast is described incorporating many of the characteristics of the other beasts mentioned there. It thus sums up all those frightening characteristics of several nations. As in Dan. 7, the Beast arises from the sea, possibly indicative of primeval chaos to which its idolatrous practices are about to reduce the world. The sea has a threatening quality in Revelation. It is of glass mingled with fire in 15.2 and has to be crossed, but is absent from the perfection of the new creation (21.1). The order brought by God in creation has been threatened. The disorder evident in the cataclysm of Revelation 6ff. is a consequence of the refusal by God to restrain any longer the forces of chaos. The creatures in rebellion put the order of the covenant at risk by their fascination with Satan, the representative of the world of chaos (9.2; 11.7).

Two creatures are described (13.1 and 11). John's inspiration may have come from the arrival of the representative of Rome by sea and the local, indigenous promoter of the worship of Rome and the emperor, of which there was a prominent example in Asia Minor. Its task was by its propaganda to encourage support for Rome. We are treated in 13.11ff. to a graphic portrait of an ideology which creates support and by its activities cloaks its real goals and identity from those it has taken in. It prompts devotion by its almost supernatural power. Many are led astray but the attentive reader of Revelation is not left in any doubt about the appropriate response.

Unlike Jesus, who in his temptation rejects power at the hands of Satan (Luke 4.6), the Beast receives this from the dragon (13.2). It is not merely the case that the Beast is given power by the dragon that brings about the worship and adulation of the earth. There is no suggestion that human beings are merely pawns determined to conform to the dictates of the Evil One. There is the active consent of humanity, for they collude with the usurpation of sovereignty which belongs to God alone. That collusion may be hinted at in the text itself. Repeatedly we are told that the Beast 'was allowed' to say and do certain things (vv. 5, 7 and 14). Such permission is from all those who collude with a diabolical system and *allow* it to wreak havoc by means of idolatrous claims and injustice. *We* are the ones who allow the process whereby institutions emerge which enable idols like Caesar and Mammon to take the place of God.

The reasons for the shortcomings of the state are laid bare. The Beast is the incarnation of the powers of the Devil ('the dragon conferred on it his own power' 13.2) and attracts universal admiration for acts which *appear* to be beneficial ('the whole world went after the Beast in wondering admiration' v. 3). The plausibility of the Beast is seen, as it is like the Lamb and appears to deserve worship. The wonder of the world is rooted in its military power (13.4). Public opinion goes along with the propaganda of the Beast and its supporters. The pressure is to conform, but that means to be marked with the mark of the Beast (13.14). Those who refuse to do so are offered reassurance that being marked with the name of the Lamb is a sign of righteousness even if it means social ostracism (13.16). In the present age those marked with the Beast have freedom to go about their activities, whereas those who refuse to be so marked and side with God and the Lamb are persecuted and their deaths are greeted with glee by the inhabitants of the earth (11.10). In reality it is those who maintain their integrity, even at the price of their lives, who will be vindicated, whereas those who have the mark of the Beast 'drink the wine of God's anger' (14.10). Those who persevere (an important theme of Revelation) are shown that the might of state power is itself extraordinarily fragile, and its affluence and prestige, so attractive and alluring, is destined for destruction destroyed by precisely that power which has maintained it (as we shall see when we look at 17.16).

The Beast has some of the characteristics of the Lamb (13.3 and 14)

in possessing the marks of death. It is easy to confuse the way of the
Beast and the way of the Messiah (cf. Matt. 24.5, 11 and 24). So
watchfulness is essential to avoid being taken in by false messiahs
and end up supporting injustice and oppression. It is necessary to
test the convictions of those who proclaim that they stand for Christ
when in reality they stand for the system of the Beast. Superficially
they may seem to belong to the way of the Messiah, but closer
inspection will reveal something very different. The maintenance of
civilization, of family, nation and property in the name of Christ is
blasphemy. It cannot be squared with the way of the Lamb. That is
because it too quickly *excludes* the deprived. It puts nation and
privilege above human community and the right to possess above
the privilege of serving. In Revelation the nation is subordinated to
the international 'multitude which no one could number' (7.9). That
multitude comes from *every* nation.

The enigmatic number referred to at the end of this chapter has, of
course, been the subject of much speculation. John may have been
inspired by the story circulating in his day that the Emperor Nero
would come back to life and lead an army from the east'.[1] Both
Hebrew and Greek use letters for numbers, a = 1, b = 2 etc. The
numerical value of letters was a field of study popular among the
Jews especially. The numerical value of Nero Caesar *in Hebrew* is 666.
Also possible is the fact that 666 three times falls short of the number
of perfection 7, while Jesus in Greek adds up to 888, one who is
beyond all human concepts of perfection (see p. 17 above). The Beast
seems to be near perfection but in fact is diabolical and utterly
opposed to God in supposing that it has ultimate power and wisdom
(13.4). We are probably right to refuse to be tied down to one possible
interpretation of this enigmatic passage.

The similarity of the Beast to Christ raises another issue. Frequently we are faced with the situation of two mutually exclusive
claims to Christian practice. Revelation at first sight seems to suggest
that the choice between them is clear. The temptation is to suppose
that there must be a bit of truth in both positions and look for some
compromise. Revelation however, beckons us to pause before we
reach that conclusion.

We should not underestimate the effect of a prevailing set of ideas
to form our minds so that when something different and challenging
comes along we consider it 'wrong'. That is exactly the function of

---

[1] Suetonius, *Life of Nero* 57.

ideology.[2] It makes you think that the ideas which are widely held are 'obvious', 'commonsense' and 'normal' when in fact they often cover up the powerful vested interests of a small group which has and wants to retain power. In John's vision the task of the second beast from the land is to persuade ordinary people that what they see in the first beast is normal and admirable, so that any deviation or counter-attraction is regarded as strange and to be repudiated. John's vision helps to unmask these processes and challenges the view that the majority opinion must always be right and to be copied (13.3 and 8).

There has been a tendency to limit the applicablity of Rev. 13 either to an eschatological manifestation of evil or to the specific case of tyrannous regimes which demand complete obedience from their subjects. Rom. 13 is then left as the mainstream New Testament teaching on the state with its apparent exhortation to be subject. Such a limitation of the applicability of Rev. 13 limits the breadth of the New Testament witness, however. What Rev. 13 brings out most clearly is the *demonic* character of the state. State or society is not a neutral enterprise devoid of conflict of interest or human self-aggrandizement. Political theorists from Hobbes to Marx have shown how the state is a means of controlling or masking deep-seated conflicts of interest, and it is important that structures of society are subjected to the same searching critique in the light of Christ as individual morality. Revelation bids us do just that. As human agents we are prone to use power (or acquiescence by our lack of resolve) in promoting institutions which will serve individual or sectional interests. That can soon lead to blasphemy when they do not acknowledge the interest of God. That does not merely mean a nod in the direction of religion but a substantial practical implementation of ways of behaving and the attempt to create institutions which will give effect to the goals of God's justice.

At least indirectly, Rom. 13 makes a similar point. The blanket injunction to be subject is qualified by the assertion that the powers are there as God's agents 'working for your good' (Rom. 13.4). Whatever the source of Paul's teaching on the state, the understanding of the good in this context must surely be informed by the wider Pauline context where the divine goodness has been mentioned several times, particularly in Rom. 12.12. It is true that Paul

[2] See the discussion in Terry Eagleton, *Ideology. An Introduction*, Routledge, Chapman and Hall 1991.

does *not* say: 'submit to the powers *only* if they promote your good'. Nevertheless Rom. 13 may outline an ideal view of the state which needs to be qualified by the more realistic portrayal in Rev. 13. The latter indicates that states always serve the interests of some and not of all, and, in particular, states approve of those who consent to their beliefs and practices. Whatever our views about the precise character of the doctrine of original sin as expounded by Augustine, its emphasis on the all-pervasive character of sin and its effects on human society demands of Christians a critical distance from all human projects. That does not mean a fatalistic acceptance that everything is going to be flawed and that projects for change are not worth bothering with since they are bound to fail. Nor should it lead us to suppose that there is an 'apolitical' place. There is nowhere in the world where conflict of interest does not intrude. It is necessary to engage in those projects knowing that human desire, acquisitiveness and self-seeking can distort the most altruistic and well-meaning cause for its own ends:

> Spirit of truth and judgement,
> who alone can exorcize
> the powers that grip our world:
> at the point of crisis
> give us your discernment,
> that we may accurately discern what is evil,
> and know the way that leads to peace,
> through Jesus Christ, Amen.[3]

Idolatry

Already in the letters to the seven churches the Risen Christ challenged those who would be tempted to idolatry (2.14). In this case the eating of food sacrificed to idols is the issue. The clear denunciation of this practice contrasts somewhat with what Paul had to say in I Cor. 8 (though it needs to be said that he is unequivocal in his repudiation of idolatry in I Cor. 10). Paul had agreed with the strong faction in Corinth that there was no reality in an idol and that food would not recommend the believer to God. He only asked them to remember the consciences of the 'weaker' in the community and not

---

[3] Janet Morley, *All Desires Known*, p. 11.

to cause them to stumble. The prohibition against idolatry is a recognition of the close link between religious practice and beliefs and patterns of behaviour in wider society. A narrowing of the sphere of religion would have been difficult for a Jew to comprehend. Rejection of idolatry in the Old Testament is bound up with a counter-cultural attitude of holiness in which a whole way of life is rejected in favour of the worship and practice of Yahwism. The struggle against Canaanite religion represented by the Baals when Israel settled in Canaan was a struggle to maintain the identity of Israel as a holy, covenant people rather than merely be submerged in the local culture.[4] Of course, that rigid separation justified what seem to us horrific barbarism in the ruthless extermination of populations (cf. Deut. 23.9ff.; Josh. 8; I Sam. 21.5; II Sam. 11.11; Lev. 15.16). In all this there is a reminder of the deep-rooted fear of the gradual assimilation of a minority group by a dominant culture, something which became reality during the Solomonic empire.

In Rev. 13 the issue of idolatry is linked with the acceptance of a way of life in which the mark of the Beast extends to every department of life (13.17). In this chapter the classic symptom of idolatry is to be found: 'man is the measure of all things'. God's place is usurped; the creatures worship another creature (13.15). The thing about the idol is that it has some of the characteristics of the one who deserves worship and honour (13.14). It is part of of the role of the book of Revelation to point out what is true worship by means of the honour offered to God in the heavenly court.

In the wilderness the people of Israel worshipped the Golden Calf (Ex. 32) and were shown what idolatry involved. Instead of the unseen God who went before them they wanted something dazzling and static, a *tangible* expression which accommodated itself to their desires. The calf was their creation. An idol embodies our desires which we then project outside ourselves and indulge in self-gratification in the belief that we worship God. The idol is the work of our hands to which we attribute a quasi-divine, mystical status and suppose that it represents something other than ourselves when it merely embodies our desires. Idolatry panders to our desire to be in close touch with God, to satisfy us that there is something other than us, but it offers us a divinity we can touch and (apparently) control. It can be argued that one of the problems with the theology of Isa. 40–

[4] See further Alan Kreider, *Journey towards Holiness. A Way of Living for God's Nation*, Marshall Pickering 1986.

55 is that the picture of God offered there is *so* transcendent that our puniness and insignificance becomes all the more evident. Yet that needs to be set alongside concerns expressed in Isa. 43.1f. (discussed above, pp. 109ff.). Similarly the glorious vision of God in Rev. 4 is accompanied by the vision of Christ standing in the midst of the churches encouraging and reproaching: the Word is very near you (cf. Rom. 10.8). A Christianity which stresses God's transcendence opens the door to idolatry by denying the immanence and warmth which we need without allowing our desires and aspirations to be identified with God.

When we indulge desires to the extent that we suppose that they represent the sum of all that is, then we lose all critical perspective and God who stands over against us and who confronts us with obligations is ignored. The point is well made by the German philosopher Max Horkheimer:

> The concept of God was for a long time the place where the idea was kept alive that there are other norms besides those to which nature and society give expression ... Dissatisfaction with earthly destiny is the strongest motivation for acceptance of a transcendent being. If justice registers with God, then it is not found in the same measure in the world. Religion is the record of the wishes, desires and accusations of countless generations.[5]

We need our desires to be set in the context of the world of which we are a part, so that we avoid self-centredness. That is the problem of Mammon, so roundly repudiated by Jesus. Our modern translations miss the point if we suppose that Jesus is merely talking about money. It is money as an idol. The work of our hands achieves a mystical quality with superhuman characteristics which displaces God. Nowhere in our contemporary language is this more evident than the way in which we ascribe almost supernatural quality to 'the market'. A place of exchange between human agents is given superhuman status with a life of its own, beyond our control. In such situations the idols have to be unmasked and knocked down from their pedestals. Isaiah of the exile (in Isa. 40–55) does this with his ridicule of idolatrous practices. We need to be told that what we regard as sacred and beyond our control and needing to appease is *in the first instance* a human creation. It has become demonic and demands our subservience. Of course, we do become enslaved by

[5] M. Horkheimer, *Critical Theory*, ET, Continuum 1972, p. 129.

the works of our hands and trapped by the deceit needed to sustain the whole web of injustice. The poor can continue to be poor and oppressed in the service of that which is no god because of the apparently unchanging laws demanded by the idol. To continue in this way is to build shrines and burn our sons and daughters to Moloch (cf. Jer. 7.31). The idol's desires are endless because it embodies the insatiable demand of ourselves for our own satisfaction The maintenance of idolatry is self-serving and exclusive of the interest of others. It is the quintessential expression of special interests. Revelation, like Old Testament prophecy, refuses to baptize the world as it is and accept the values of the surrounding culture.

We need to recognize that whenever Christianity has set itself up as the dominant, oppressive religious system, those who are victims of it have sometimes kept their own identity by subverting it. In the Afro-Brazilian religions, for example, the slaves from Africa kept their past alive by identifying aspects of the Christian religion forced upon them with their ancestral gods. That, in my view, is very different from the syncretistic process described in the Old Testament. There it is the élite of Judean society which was responsible for making the life of the nation conform to the values of the surrounding culture. In the reforms which are reported under Hezekiah (II Kings 18.4ff.) it is the cleansing of the temple of idolatrous clutter that symbolizes a change of heart on the part of the royal court and the priesthood. Nevertheless, as Jer. 7 indicates, such a task will not 'unclutter' the mind and outlook of a people whose whole way of life is inbred with idolatry. During the period of Solomon's temple the opposition to idolatry came from outsiders, from Amos, Hosea and those who preserved the Mosaic ideal as represented in the book of Deuteronomy. The subversion of the *status quo* is what the worship of almighty God leads to, according to the book of Revelation. It was an exile on Patmos who exposed so comprehensively the lies and deceit involved in maintaining obedience to the Beast and the wealth of Babylon. Purity of worship is only part of the solution to the problem of idolatry. It requires a change of heart which will mean ceasing to oppress the poor (Micah 2.1ff.; 6.9ff.). Idolatry represents a life that is completely submerged in the economic and cultural life of the present so that it cannot see that is forfeiting its own soul (cf. Luke 12.15ff.).

The followers of the Lamb and of the Beast
14–15

As with ch. 7, where the sealing of the elect contrasted with the judgement on an unjust world, so ch. 14 offers a contrast with the previous chapter. Those who conform to the ways of the Beast may achieve a temporary respite and prosperity but it is ephemeral. John's vision here offers a firm promise to those who stand firm (14.1, 12). The two characteristics of the 144,000 are that no lie was found on their lips and they were without fault (14.5). That stress on integrity and truthfulness contrasts with the duplicity and deceit manifest in the previous chapter. What is false (13.14) leads astray and is met by self-deception and the self-seeking response of the world's inhabitants. Those who have compromised realize the error of their ways as the truth is revealed (14.6). The vision brings home the ultimate character of apparently harmless actions. The odd bit of compromise with the old order is nothing less than being marked by the Beast (14.9). It is not good enough to say 'we were only doing our duty' or 'I had to look after my family and my interests; what else could I do?' No, the message is clear, however uncomfortable. Maintenance of injustice and disorder at the expense of integrity, truth and injustice cannot be tolerated and will reap its own reward (14.15ff.). It can only in the end lead to misery, death and destruction; God's righteousness and truth will ultimately prevail.

Those marked with the name of the Lamb are chaste (14.4). Like the Old Testament warriors who, when engaging in a holy war, remained pure (Deut. 21.10f.), so too these saints are ones who maintain their holiness. It may well be the case that we should interpret the celibacy here metaphorically as indicative of refusal to compromise with an unjust social order. It is the element of cost and service which casts light on the exclusive focus on men in this passage. There is nothing else in Revelation to suggest that the community of the elect is made up only of men. Indeed, 7.9 implicitly suggests the contrary. Just as the 144,000 represents the full complement of the people of God (cf. Rom. 11.25), a number of perfection

(12 x 12), so the character of those called is described in terms of the preparation necessary for the holy war. Those who engage in warfare (Deut. 20 and 23) have to be in a state of holiness which meant, according to the law, avoidance of sexual intercourse (Lev. 15.16). As in Eph. 6.10, we are offered in Rev. 14 a picture of a battle conducted without weapons of war and rooted in the triumph of the Lamb (14.1) who, like the Messiah in the contemporary apocalypse IV Ezra (13.10, 27), stands as a conqueror without engaging in any military action. The warfare of the elect is conducted with other weapons: endurance, witness, prophecy, obedience to God and remaining loyal to Jesus (14.12). We should recall that Jesus points out to Pilate that if his kingdom was to be understood by the standards of the old order his followers would fight (John 18.36).

The contrast between Revelation and the War Scroll (IQM) from the Dead Sea Scrolls is in this respect quite remarkable. In one of the most fascinating texts found in the vicinity of the Dead Sea we find in minute detail the inventory of preparations necessary for the fight between the sons of light and sons of darkness. This is a conventional battle in that weapons of war are used. Like Revelation it is apparent that this battle is one that is not confined to humans but also involves angelic forces (cf. Josh. 5.14). Unlike Revelation, however, it countenances an active role in the violence which is necessary to destroy the sons of darkness.

The passage stands in a long tradition of ascetic practice where its *social* as well as religious importance should be noted. In a world of affluence on the one hand and enormous suffering and deprivation on the other, and where there are limited choices available to take a stand on the way things are, renunciation offers an important avenue.[1] The vocation of renunciation is one that Christian women, who have particular experience of exclusion and oppression, have taken both as a way of discipleship and a means of self-affirmation in a male-dominated world.[2] It is not the repudiation of the body that is important. Virginity is honoured because distance from family meant distance from the normal pattern of society (I Cor. 7.32ff. – chastity is the subject of I Cor. 7) and commitment to a different way of being community (Mark 3.34f.).

[1] See Peter Brown, *Body and Society: Men, Women, and Sexual Renunciation in Early Christianity*, Faber and Faber 1990; R. Lane Fox, *Pagans and Christians*, Viking Press 1986, particularly the chapter 'Living like Angels'.
[2] Rosemary R. Reuther and E. McLaughlin, eds., *Women of Spirit: Female Leadership in the Jewish and Christian Traditions*, Simon and Schuster 1979.

The manifestation of the elect (cf. Rom. 8.19) is accompanied by heaven's proclamation of the true object of worship (14.7) and the prediction of the destruction of Babylon, that wonderful city of the Beast on which humanity had set its hope (13.14). The command of the angel to fear God and give God the glory is a challenge to repudiate forbidden things (cf. Josh. 7.19 and the use of this text also in John 9.24). The manifestation of the elect offers a final test as a result of the proclamation of an eternal gospel, but the folly of darkened minds will not own its misguidedness.

The contrast between the two ways of life is made most clearly in the third angelic speech in 14.9: worship of the Beast and possession of its mark means eternal torment. The elect have the Lamb's and God's names written on their foreheads (14.1; cf. 22.4); they are truly reflecting God's image and character. They stand with the Lamb, a position that is not easily gained or maintained. This calls for endurance, therefore, which is rooted in 'keeping God's commands and remaining loyal to Jesus' (14.12). The elect are assured that what they have done will not be forgotten (14.13).

The chapter concludes with an anticipation of the picture of judgement, reaffirming the awesome nature of the decisions taken here and now. The passage is rich in scriptural themes (e.g. Isa. 63.2). This passage alongside 19.7ff. is a gruesome reminder of the terrible nature of judgement and nothing can be offered by way of explanation to reduce its horrific brutality. We may feel disgust that the loving and merciful God could indulge in such an orgy of destruction and barbarity. Indeed, God seems to descend to the level of barbarism of the creatures who are being judged. That is a reality which reading Revelation demands that we wrestle with. The passage stresses the importance in any Christian doctrine of a God of justice; it is God who judges, not humans. The heavenly hymns in chs. 15 and 16 laud the just character of that judgement (e.g. 15.3ff.). The message is of vindication of the ways of divine justice and it is by that criterion that human projects or individuals will be judged. It is not strictly a vindictive attitude that is manifest here (though that is hinted at at various points elsewhere, e.g. 6.9; 16.6; 19.3). The occasional evidence of 'gloating' over the fate of the damned should not be overemphasized. Like the passages in the Psalms which call for the vindication of the righteous and vengeance on the wicked, they are an honest recognition of the human heart's desires. How we deceive ourselves if we deny that we ever feel thus! But they are *occasional* flashes of vindictiveness and are not part of God's own comment on the eschatological drama. If the new age is characterized by the quenching of thirst and the wiping away of tears (7.16; 21.4), the absence of these activities from the priorities of the old order have to be remedied, and in the face of resistance to them and the way of the Lamb, the implementation of that practice manifests itself as wrath. It is on the face of it a harsh and unpalatable message.

It is hard, when in the middle of a commitment to a set of principles or to a particular community, to maintain the balance between integrity and compassion. Those who are committed to causes continually need to ask themselves about that commitment, their motives in making it and the cost to others and to themselves. The first fruits of redemption (14.4) cannot pursue the good cause without self-criticism. In such circumstances it may seem easier to decide that nothing justifies the cost that Revelation expects to be paid. Yet it has ever been the case that simple concern for humanity and the protest against that which demeans has brought with it cost for those who have taken that path. Suffering is not an end in itself. The way of the cross was not one that was taken because it led to suffering, but because God's reign and its benefits for humanity demanded it (Luke 13.34).

The following words of Sister Edmée of the Society of the Love of God deserve to be pondered:

> ... it is precisely in becoming identified with a cause that one may betray it ... the ego is aroused and attaches itself to a particular cause ... it will then be the ego, now identified with this cause, which works on its behalf. Such identification is the antithesis of poverty of spirit, and these are its signs: it is elated by success, cast down by failure, enraged by criticism, sustained by self-righteousness. It engages in acrimonious controversy, does not restrain itself from scoring debating points, even in matters of life and death, and seizes even its sympathizers by the throat – down which it thrusts its message. Finally, at the end of a very hard day, it retires into its corner sobbing with self-pity ...

There is, however. a temptation never to take sides and find something of good in every position; consequently a stand is never taken about anything. Of course, certainty of the rectitude of one's cause can lead to intransigence and a mindless devotion to the cause. One can think of many 'causes'. How does one judge between them?

With which does the Lamb identify? Does Revelation have any light to shed on such questions?

Two things seem to stand out. First of all, there is a clear repudiation of special interest for oneself when this means abandoning the ways of God. Secondly, that is given more precision in ch. 14 because the elect are seen not on their own but standing with the Lamb. It is the Lamb who stands on Mount Zion accompanied by those who had his name and God's name on their foreheads. The criterion of the good cause must be the person, activity and story of the Lamb. As Paul would put it, it must be conformity with the mind of Christ that counts. Of course, this is no infallible guide. But in the light of this it is difficult to justify the cause of hanging on to wealth and privilege. That was not the way of the Messiah. The exaltation of the state, family and property sits very uneasily with the story of one who died for treason, redefined the identity of the family (Mark 3.34f.; Luke 4.26) and had strong words to say about Mammon (Matt. 6.24).

For John *all* action, however small, is ultimately significant and of infinite value in the divine economy. The significance of human behaviour is expressed clearly in ch. 15. Victory over the beast (15.2) is a metaphor of non-conformity and refusal to accept its dominion and way of life. That action becomes equivalent to the redemptive crossing of that threatening sea to God's side. The apparently 'innocent' act of not conforming by burning a pinch of incense to the genius of Caesar is the moment of traversing the threatening sea. The neutral, secular action is an event of supreme importance in the eyes of God, almost on a par with that fundamental redemptive moment in Israel's history. The redemptive moment means siding with the Lamb at the moment of testimony and standing firm in one's convictions and commitment to the horizon of hope symbolized by the Lamb who bears the marks of slaughter.

When the people of Israel reached the other side of the Red Sea they sang a song of deliverance (Ex. 15). That is echoed in Rev. 15. The sea of glass which John had seen in heaven in Rev. 4 now has a threatening quality, just as the Red Sea seemed to trap the people as Pharaoh's army advanced upon them. Those who were victorious against the Beast, its image and the number of its name (15.2), sing a song of deliverance. They are the ones who could pass through the threat posed by the sea of glass mingled with fire and attain to God's presence because their defender and leader was the Lamb (14.1). Like the slaves who escaped from Egypt with nothing but trust in

God and God's justice, so those who maintain their cause can expect to pass through the threat posed by the manifestation of God's justice (the sanctuary of the heavenly Tent of Testimony symbolizes that justice and judgement). Exodus themes are prominent throughout Revelation. In addition to this chapter, 1.6 (cf. Ex. 19.16); 1.8 (cf. Ex. 3.14); 2.17 (cf. Ex. 16 and the manna); chs. 6–8 (cf. the plagues in Ex. 7–11) should all be noted.

The justice of divine judgement is brought out in the final verses of ch. 15. The seven last plagues (15.1) bring about the final sequence of seven. Their origin is in the tabernacle of witness in heaven (15.5). That Tent of Testimony is the storage place of God's covenant obligations (Ex. 40.34). It evokes the dread holiness of Isa. 6.4 where the house filled with smoke. The temple has been mentioned previously. In 7.15 it is the location of the eternal service of the elect. Of more relevance to this passage is 11.19, where the manifestation of the heavenly temple and the ark of the Lord forms the climax of the vindication of the testimony of the two witnesses. There the ark of the covenant is explicitly mentioned and the giving of the law at Sinai recalled (Ex. 19.16).

The connection between the seven plagues and God is made even closer. The exclusion of all from the temple until the completion of the seven last plagues seems to highlight their importance as the locus of attention. It is the covenant which forms the basis of the case against human infidelity and disobedience. The basis for the vindication of the witnesses and the judgement of their persecutors is set in God's covenant. That is backed up by both of the celestial hymns sung in 15.3ff. and 11.17ff. (cf. 16.5ff). In 15.3ff. God's ways are hailed as just and true. In the latter, God's decision to manifest divine sovereignty by vindicating those who are faithful suggests that John's visionary consciousness does have a dim awareness of the destructiveness to the earth caused by humanity. The destruction is the result of the abrogation of a covenant in which the balance between heaven and earth, animal and human, men and women, has been distorted by sin.[3]

---

[3] See further R. Murray, *The Cosmic Covenant*, Sheed and Ward 1992, for an excellent discussion of the cosmic and societal consequences of the derogation of God's covenant.

The last seven plagues: the bowls of God's wrath

16

The sequence of the consequences of the opening of the seals, the blowing of the trumpets and the pouring of the celestial bowls have already been tabulated (above p. 82). In the sequence of the last plagues (cf. 15.1) there are, interspersed with the tale of judgement, comments by the angel of the waters (16.5), a voice from the altar (16.7) and an isolated statement, apparently from Christ (16.15, cf. Matt. 24.43; I Thess. 5.2; Rev. 1.3):

First bowl, on earth: sores on those who worship the beast.

Second bowl, on sea: the sea becomes blood and every creature in it dies.

Third bowl, on rivers and springs: they become blood.

An *angelic proclamation* about God's justice, that blood is to be drunk by those who shed the blood of God's people and prophets.

Fourth bowl, on the sun: humanity scorched; they blasphemed the name of God and did not repent (cf. 9.20; 14.7 and 15.4).

Fifth bowl, on the throne of the Beast: its kingdom darkened; people gnaw their tongues in agony, blaspheme and do not repent.

Sixth bowl, on the Euphrates: it is dried up to prepare for kings from east; three unclean spirits from the Beast gather the kings of the world for Armageddon.

Saying: Behold I come like a thief.

Seventh bowl, on the air: an earthquake; a third of the great city falls; the people curse God.

Terrible afflictions continue to dominate John's picture of the reality of the unjust life of humanity. A link is made in the first plague with the judgement on those who have the mark of the Beast (16.1). The plagues affect different parts of the created world. Once again the unfolding of the process of divine wrath is interspersed with angelic proclamations of God's just judgements (16.5). The seventh bowl is accompanied by a voice from the throne marking the completion of the process which is accompanied by that array of theophanic signs accompanying the giving of the covenant (4.5; 11.19; cf. Ex. 19.16). The proclamation of the heavenly voice is reminiscent of John 19.30, where Jesus says, at the moment of his death, 'It is accomplished'. The completion of the eschatological tribulation and wrath and the death of Christ reminds us of the significance attached to Christ's death by early Christian writers. It was the moment of triumph over the powers of darkness (cf. Col. 2.14f.). The cruel death of Jesus has laid bare the reality of tribulation suffered by most of the world's population. It marks God's resounding 'no' to the practices of the old order. God has in Christ sided with the victims. God is taking up his reign (11.15, 17). For those who identify themselves with the Lamb, the tribulations are not a disaster but a sign of hope and justice.

In addition to the comments from heaven on the judgements, a warning precedes the seventh bowl, which appears to be more obviously directed to the churches. In words reminiscent of Christ in 1.3 (cf. I Thess. 5.2), blessedness is proclaimed on those who watch and keep their clothes at hand so that they are not found naked (cf. Mark 13.33 and 37; Mark 14.34; Matt. 25.5). 'Beatitudes' are a feature of Revelation as well as the Sermon on the Mount, see 1.3; 14.13; 16.15; 19.9; 20.6; 22.7, 14. The fear of nakedness which informs other parts of the book (3.18; cf. 6.9 and 17.16), is that same fear of eschatological nakedness that may lie behind II Cor. 5, where Paul speaks about his deep longing to put on 'a house not made with human hands'. Whether what is stored up in heaven is a heavenly, resurrection body, or the heavenly temple or house which swallows up the elect as it descends from heaven, is unclear. There does seem to be expressed a deep anxiety that after going before Christ's judgement seat (II Cor. 5.10) Paul might find himself naked rather than clothed (like the unrepentant Laodiceans or desolate Babylon). The sense of shame alluded to here is shame at having the reality of oneself revealed for what it is and one's deeds uncovered (cf. 14.13). When the secrets will be disclosed where shall we find cover (cf. 6.16)?

In 14.7 and 15.4 (cf. 11.13) the heavenly voices had implied that humanity might just see the error of its ways. Both verses seem to hold hope of people coming to their senses, give God the glory and acknowledge God as Creator. That hope now evaporates. In 9.20 there had been a wholly negative reaction to the first sequence of divine wrath. Now there is a threefold repetition of human blasphemy (16.9; 16.11; 16.21). There is no recognition of the

127

works which had brought such evil to the world (16.11: 'they did not repent of their works'). There are no overwhelming proofs which compel repentance. The parables in Mark's Gospel are comments on rejection and misunderstanding (3.22ff. and 4.1ff.) and are meant to bring enlightenment but end up causing blindness (Mark 4.12). Likewise the manifestation of the wrath of the Lamb should lead to repentance. Instead humanity blasphemes God. The blame for the chaos of the world is put on God and there is no awareness that human sinfulness may have brought about this disruption. Fear and homage to the God of heaven (11.13) cannot be a substitute for a change in one's works (9.20). In 16.8 there is not even a willingness to do God homage, only the cursing and blaspheming which comes from a refusal to recognize responsibility for destroying the earth (11.18).

'This calls for a mind with insight'
17

Amidst the chaos of destruction attention now focusses on Babylon. Few commentators would want to deny that at the time when John was writing Rome had inspired his views (hence the reference to seven hills in 17.9). The image can be of universal application because of the description of the city as Babylon, a symbol of military power and oppression (cf. Isa. 13.6; 21.1; Jer. 5.17), even if the immediate inspiration may have been the might of Rome.[1] It also was the place of exile and alienation (Ps. 137 and I Peter 5.13) where the people of God do not feel at home and are always exiles.

John is taken to a desert place (17.3; cf.21.10). That desert place is one that allows Babylon to be seen for what it is. The wilderness is a place for seeing things in their proper perspective (cf. Hosea 2.14) untrammelled by the lures of surrounding culture and the intoxication of power which seem so overwhelming. The stark clarity of the iniquity and character of Babylon and its relationship with the Beast can be seen for what they really are.

This chapter is unusual in Revelation because of the deliberate historical allusions which are to be found in 17.8ff. These verses were a central item in the discussion of the date of Revelation (see the Introduction, pp. 17). Once again we note in 17.11 a possible allusion to the legend that Nero who had died would come to life again.[2] The Roman historian Tacitus tells us that Nero persecuted Christians in Rome, laying responsibility for the great fire in 64 on their shoulders. Within this context we are reminded that the imagery relates to the realities of flesh and blood, not to some 'science fiction' scene which is only the creation of the mind of the author. This chapter stresses that the leading political and economic power of John's day is infected with an outlook and practice that is

---

[1] See further K. Wengst, *Pax Romana and the Peace of Jesus Christ*, ET, SCM Press 1987.
[2] See Suetonius, *Life of Nero* 57.

opposed to God and destined to destruction. That outspoken view of the Pharaohs of our world is not very palatable to a church which likes to see the best in everyone and every thing and to be on equally good terms with all. What the vision leaves no doubt about is the hostility of a state where self-satisfaction and self-aggrandizement are the order of the day, in opposition to the way of the Lamb (17.14).

The description of the woman sets up several contrasts with the Bride of the Lamb, the new Jerusalem, e.g. 17.1, cf. 21.9; 17.4, cf. 21.19, 24. The golden cup in her hand is full of abominations (17.4). The word used is the same as the manifestation of evil used in Mark 13.14, cf. Matt. 24.15. The Danielic background (Dan. 11.31) suggests idolatry. Babylon is depicted as a whore with whom the kings of the earth commit fornication and get drunk with the wine of Babylon's fornication (17.2). Babylon in turn is drunk from the blood of the saints (17.6). The mighty of the earth are intoxicated by her power and their collaboration is so intimate that it can only be described in sexual terms. Babylon's intoxication is such that it results in the deaths of saints and martyrs who refuse to be taken in. Harlotry involves selling one's body. It is that intimate union for the financial benefit of one and the gratification of the other party which offers this metaphor of illicit collaboration rooted in self-satisfaction and loss of human dignity. Babylon has grown wealthy and powerful because of 'fornication'.

We have seen how clear-cut contrasts are very much part of the way in which Revelation interprets reality. Thus there is a strong compulsion throughout Revelation to avoid compromise and the blurring of boundaries. Sexual intercourse brought about unclean-ness (Lev. 15 and 18), and this link is taken up in 18.2. If intercourse involves consummation, which ought to come only when the marriage of God and the bride takes place in the new age, then inter-course before then (cf. 14.4) is likely to be precipitate. 'Fornication' represents confusion and unnecessary compromise with the old order.

Fornication in the Old Testament is a metaphor for idolatry. In Hosea 1–2 it is used of the practices of Israel. Israel is seen as an unfaithful wife (Hosea 2.2) whose idolatrous practices have caused her to stray from God's way. It is symptomatic of that lack of distinctiveness in religious practice and social organization which is the result of a settled life-style. Israel has become like the nations. What better way to describe this than fornication? It is the abrogation of the covenant, just as adultery and fornication are a deliberate ignoring of the marriage contract. Fornication elsewhere in Revelation is a metaphor for compromise with the surrounding culture which is unacceptable (2.14; 2.20). In 2.20 the 'lovers' of Jezebel are clearly the adherents of that teaching. The kings of the earth commit involvement in trade with Babylon which enables its great, indeed obscene, wealth. Even ordinary people have some benefit provided they become part of the system. They can get drunk with the wine of Babylon's fornication, unlike the kings who commit fornication themselves with Babylon. The picture we are offered is of people so stupefied by their participation in Babylon's activities that they are in no state of mind to see clearly the cost in human lives which makes Babylon great.

Babylon is supported (17.3) by a whole régime whose outlook is idolatrous (ch. 13) and therefore the whole complex of relationships is shot through with the tainted practices and a distorted pattern of behaviour, particularly evident in the way in which the Lamb and its followers are the targets for hostility (17.14). The vision of Babylon seated on many waters (17.1, 15) supported by the Beast (17.2) is inherently unstable. The waters are the myriad of nations (17.15) from whom the elect come (5.9). Resting on water and a Beast, Babylon is destined for collapse and destruction (17.16). That which has caused intoxication and power will itself be turned on and destroyed. Babylon will be seen in her pitiable state of nakedness (17.16), just as the reality of the Laodicean church's life is shown up for what it really is (3.17). In Hosea 2.3 and 2.9 nakedness is the judgement of God on an unrepentant people. There it seems to be conceived of as the devastation of her economy with the result that all those who have been Israel's 'lovers' will see her poverty (2.9). In similar vein God will allow Babylon's poverty to be seen for what it really is. Her wealth and 'false' clothes mask her need and destitution.

The reader is enabled to understand how the wealth of Babylon comes by ways other than those which God's justice requires. It comes at the expense of millions (particularly 18.13). It is a telling reminder that the world power is an oppressor and a place of exile, not one of comfort and real prosperity. It may seem to the nations of the world that they have achieved great prosperity as a result of Babylon's power (18.3), but in God's estimation things are very different.

The description of Babylon (together with the account of its wealth) owes much to Ezek. 27–28 (the prophecy against Tyre) and

Jer. 51. The passage from Ezekiel is particularly important. There the emphasis is on the economic activity and success of Tyre. The description of the city's greatness revolves around its role as a centre of trade. It is this element that is to the fore in chs. 17 and 18, with the long lists of goods which are part of the commerce which Babylon's greatness encouraged. The goods are in large part luxuries, hardly the basic necessities which formed the subsistence of most people in John's (or in our) day (Rev. 18.11ff.; cf. Ezek. 27.12ff.). Tyre was a centre of trade. The description of Babylon in 17.4 suggests conspicuous *consumption*. The 'harlotry' points to the illicit wealth and the self-indulgence involved at a cost to the many parts of the world which were drained of goods and resources.[3] Luxury goods gravitate to the centre to supply its insatiable needs. It has the effect of making the rest of the world peripheral. Those on the periphery become merely means of supplying the needs of others.

The woman who is drunk with the blood of God's people (17.6) is seated on the Beast (17.7f.), the one which had been the means of Satan's action. We are here given a graphic picture of the true nature of the way in which wealth is created. Superficially it may seem uncontroversial, but in fact it springs from an evil intent and results in oppression. The inherent instability of this system based on injustice, oppression and self-aggrandizement is made clear in 17.15ff. The Beast 'comes to hate the whore' (17.16). All the nations which had lived in fear now come to recognize the fragility of that power. Babylon is ultimately destroyed. Self-centredness and individualism always end up in destruction because the competitive instincts cannot allow mercy in the struggle for survival.

Reservations have been rightly expressed about the negative image of woman here.[4] It may seem that woman by virtue of her sexuality has led the nations astray. We have to face squarely the male-centredness of Revelation. It glorifies the holy (male) celibate (14.4). Jezebel is a symbol of false prophecy; the New Jerusalem is portrayed merely as an adjunct of the bridegroom whose life is governed by pleasing 'him', the exaltation of celibacy and the use of sexual imagery focus is on the woman as the transgressor. The book seems to exude all those negative images of women which have done so much damage to a balanced perspective on relationships between women and men in the history of the Church.

[3] There are some helpful comments on this in R. Bauckham, *The Bible in Politics*, SCM Press 1989, pp. 85ff.
[4] E.g. Tina Pippin, *Death and Desire*, Fortress Press 1991.

The picture is more complicated, however. We need to bear in mind that the ultimate inspiration for the immoral behaviour lies with the Beast supporting the woman. Babylon is hardly a mere victim but the apocalyptic imagery stresses the complexity of oppression. Babylon is deceived and culpable, but ultimately at the mercy of the Beast. Oppressors, both rich and poor, are often themselves victims of a larger and more malevolent power.

That must be balanced by 12, where the pregnant woman symbolizes the people of God. Indeed, the contrast between pursuit by the Devil and support by the earthly embodiment of evil in ch. 17 is a positive feature: woman is not wholly ambiguous and on the side of darkness. We have to accept that a passive role is accorded to the acceptable feminine images. Yet limited activity is a mark of Revelation. 'Endurance' is a dominant characteristic. In this both men and women are not mere spectators. Their activity is focussed in faith (ch. 12.9), readiness, and the expression of their emotions (5.3ff.) and that perseverance through thick and thin which has so often been a characteristic of women's role in our disordered and oppressive world.

Towards a political theology on the basis of Revelation 13 and 17

It is often said that there are few examples of political theology in the New Testament and that we have to wait for Augustine's *City of God* for anything approaching that. While that view may in general terms be correct, Rev. 13 and 17 offer an intuitive grasp of the character of a Christian political response. Christians have ignored these chapters, to the detriment of their understanding of the relationships between the church and the world, by placing too exclusive emphasis on Rom. 13 and related passages like I Peter 2 and Titus 3.

THE CHARACTER OF THE STATE

In Rev. 13 and 17 we are offered indications of the character of State institutions. The Beast in ch. 13 represents political dominion as exemplified through various figureheads of its rule. The political character of that dominion is considered in ch. 17. In the former we are offered a picture of human rule, which takes as its model the contemporary Roman imperium. It is diabolically inspired and actively promoted as *the* dominion in the universe which attracts human adoration and complete subservience and is the basis of exploitation. In ch. 13 the Beast attracts idolatrous devotion, identification with its norms and values and the active promotion of its authority leads to the exclusion of non-conformists (13.6, cf. 11.7; 12.17; 17.14). In ch. 17 the political power supports a social system, symbolized by Babylon, whose economic system is at the hub of the world, and enables kings and the mighty to do their business and a tiny minority to live in luxury. Both Beast and Babylon are opposed to God and God's ways. In ch. 17 Babylon grows rich and powerful as the result of 'fornication'. Many of the inhabitants of the world collude with Babylon for their own advantage and collaborate in her (and their) self-aggrandizement, thereby lending support to the realm of the Beast (cf. 16.10). The message of Revelation is unequivocal in both cases: Babylon is stripped naked and destroyed by those who had given her support (17.15) and the Beast is thrown into the lake of fire (19.20).

ECONOMIC MATTERS

Ch. 17 offers a critical assessment, albeit in the suggestive imagery of the visionary, of the way in which a nation becomes rich. It invites us to consider carefully the history of our wealth, and to assess the extent to which the trading which forms a part of the business of our international order (18.13) is neutral in its inspiration and effects As Oliver O'Donovan has put it: 'Trade as much as conquest violates the integrity of communities which become dominated by the influence of the stronger trading partner.'[5] The symbol of Babylon as the great harlot with whom the kings and mighty have committed fornication suggests the lengths that are gone to in order to achieve wealth, status and power. This comes about through trade, for, as O'Donovan points out 'trade is fornication. It is a cultural promiscuity by which one power exploits and drains the resources from many others.'[6] In the extravagance and luxury of life and wealth there lie hidden the cost to human lives and societies.

What Revelation refuses to allow is a view of economic and political activity which stresses their autonomy. For all the difficulty of seeking to articulate a response to God in the complexities of

[5] O. O'Donovan, 'The Political Thought of the Book of Revelation', *Tyndale Bulletin* 37, 1986, p. 85.
[6] Loc. cit.

society and political economy, there can be no abdication of responsibility for doing that in every sphere of life. The temptation of Christian people to suppose that they can treat their religious activity as in some sense a special sphere is excluded in Revelation. Acts of trade and commerce and political processes are shown to be shot through with conflicts of interest which are of paramount importance in the concerns of religious people. Leaving politics and economics to specialists, or supposing that those areas of life are impossible to interpret in the light of the gospel, or have laws of their own, is not to be countenanced. Revelation, therefore, does not allow a view of society which accepts that it has been secularized, and can be understood in its various constituent parts without reference to God. Revelation reminds us that to suppose that there is 'a divine law' which undergirds exchange in the market place, which is not to be troubled by matters of conscience or moral issues, is repugnant to the Christian gospel. However uncomfortable and however out of their depth they might feel, Christians are obliged to read and understand the nature of what confronts them through the lens of the story of Christ. That casts its shadow over every human transaction. Nothing escapes the attention of the All-Seeing One; no activity can be regarded as morally neutral and beyond the critique of and need for redemption and the Lamb who was slain.

There are those who would want to make a distinction between private and public morality, and suggest that the bulk of the material in the New Testament relates only to the former and not the latter. There are good reasons for rejecting this. Firstly, the ethic of Jesus is the ethic of a new people of God.[7] No Jew would make that kind of public/private distinction, unless there were political pressures which made some kind of accommodation necessary. Despite what is often argued, there is nothing in the teaching of Jesus which accepts a 'two realms theology' (the realm of God = the spiritual; the realm of Caesar = the temporal). The reign of God encompasses the whole of reality and the obedience demanded applies to the whole of life. The people of God are bound to articulate 'an even better way' (I Cor. 13.1) and cannot conform entirely to the solutions of this age.

Revelation is sceptical of that which manifests itself as progress, and emphasizes protest and, if necessary, withdrawal (18.4). It

---

[7] See N. Lohfink, *Jesus and Community: the Social Dimension of Christian Faith*, ET, SPCK 1985; J.H. Yoder, *The Politics of Jesus: Vicit Agnus Noster*, Eerdmans 1972, and *The Priestly Kingdom: Social Ethics as Gospel*, University of Notre Dame Press 1984.

reminds us that in the name of efficiency and progressive affluence the lives of millions have been damaged. In our pursuit of relevance, efficiency and using the techniques of the day, the temptation is to resort to what has done that most effectively in the world at large. Revelation asks us continually whether the instruments we use to achieve our goals are as value-free as we would like to think. It criticizes a political economy geared to the satisfaction of the fortunate minority at the centre of trade. It encourages suspicion of institutions, of our motives and the ongoing questioning of the character and extent of our involvement. It reminds us that in all this we wrestle not only with flesh and blood, but also with principalities and powers. It questions what is widely assumed to be reasonable and realistic by offering a different perspective on what we understand by rationality. It roots the church in the midst of social and political protest. Its horizon of hope is not utopian, for it never offers a blue-print of how things will be. The construction of ideal societies can easily degenerate into fantastic speculation out of touch with the real world. The readers of Revelation are left in their own circumstances the task of working out what faithfulness to the testimony of Jesus might mean.

THE CHURCH IN THE WORLD

Revelation demands a realistic view of the Christian community also. It too is part of the old order and is just as much susceptible to the blandishments of this age. For this reason the church cannot expect in its own life absolute clarity and perfection of practice. It has to resist the use of force which presumes that one group is in the know and the other is not. It has to live with ambiguity while struggling to maintain its identity with the Lamb. Judgement begins with the house of God in chs. 2–3 (cf. I Peter 4.17). The response is entirely practical, even if hard and at times uncompromising. It is a measure of the assessment of worth in the divine scale of values that it is the weak and apparently unsuccessful churches of Smyrna and Philadelphia that attract Christ's praise. The heart of their success is rooted in patient endurance. It is poverty that is the mark of true wealth, for it is that which risks the least amount of involvement in that system which has trapped the kings and the mighty of the earth. The church will expect dissent, but must not capitulate to values and ways of behaving which are contrary to its profession. It will expect tension between the remnant and the whole, which has always been characteristic of the people of God, and welcome that, however uncomfortable that may be for those more closely involved with pulling the levers of power. A church which seeks to quench its prophetic spirits and makes do instead with those who proclaim a false peace has lost touch with its roots. It is only in the age to come that prophecy will vanish away (I Cor. 13.9).

The view that the State has grown rich illicitly (ch. 17) is bound to be controversial. In ch. 18, it is the mighty of the world who are in particular depicted as lamenting Babylon's downfall. The losers in this age are those vindicated in the age to come (cf. 7.14 and Luke 6.20ff.), though that pursuit of wealth at any cost sucks in many others who become part and parcel of that process of accumulation and oppression (6.15). The picture of Babylon is of an unstable order supported by the Beast with its client kings (17.3, 12). For a time only these kings give their power to the Beast and are part of the system which supports Babylon (18.9). Yet that support is only temporary. They make war with the Lamb and show their contempt of God's justice (17.14) but turn against Babylon and leave her destitute (17.16). When the wealth of a nation is based on plunder and self-interest, its supporters too will look to their own interests, even if it means destroying that which they have helped to create and support, and from which they have benefited. Such a destructive attitude is inevitable, a consequence of behaviour which has no consideration for divine justice (17.17, cf. Rom. 1.24ff.). Babylon sits on many waters which are peoples, oppressed and resentful. It is a position of insecurity not evident to those hard at work maintaining it. It is only those who see their true destiny and keep their integrity by their distance from Babylon (18.4) who will maintain the possibility of another way of social organization. This points to the new Jerusalem which is dependent on God and in which every inhabitant possesses God's name and is of equal value. The kings may bring their tribute but have no privileged position. The distortions and iniquities which defiled Babylon (18.2) are absent from the new age (21.27).

DISTINCTIONS OF POLITICAL JUDGEMENT

In assessing the significance of these chapters for a political theology, the question must first be asked: do they apply to every state or are they applicable only to totalitarian regimes? It could be argued on the basis of Revelation itself that the kingdom of the Beast was not

137

always tyrannical and only gradually became so. The Beast which comes from the abyss is not mentioned until 11.7 and, at length for the first time, after the ejection of Satan from heaven in ch. 13. But that is the reality of the world order which confronts God: the triumph of God symbolized by the reigning Lamb and the demonstration of divine sovereignty (11.15ff.) show up the institutions of the world for what they are. In John's situation there was little opportunity to exercise discrimination between various forms of state power. A political critique which was formed by the marginal rather than those wielding power at the centre would have been difficult. Revelation is extant as a testimony to that voice of protest. It is an important relic of that alternative perspective from the ancient world.

It could be argued, therefore, that John's vision of the world paints with too broad a brush and fails to distinguish adequately between liberal democracy and totalitarianism. It is, of course, imperative that we do not indulge in simplistic rhetoric about injustice as if it were all of the same kind. The monstrosities of Hitler, Stalin, and Pol Pot are of a different order of magnitude from abuses in more mature democracies. That is no argument to stop the protests against the latter, but to make the criticism proportionate to the abuse suspected.

There is a fundamental point about the message of Revelation which should inform a Christian political theology. The New Testament perspective of which Revelation is an example is looking forward to the Kingdom of God and its anticipation, however partial, in the Body of Christ. Thus, any kind of arrangement which demands absolute conformity, or actions which are incompatible with the way of the Messiah, and penalizes those who deviate, must be questioned by those whose citizenship is from heaven (Phil. 3.20).

NON-CONFORMITY AND NATIONALISM

There must be in the Christian witness a thread of non-conformity. Some compromise may be inevitable (perhaps more than Revelation would care to countenance) but that cannot be allowed to degenerate into the kind of identification with and support for state power which results in the 'baptizing' of rulers and institutions of this age. There is another instinct in Revelation's portrayal of political power which is of wider applicability: the tendency of states to demand of their citizens *at some point in their history* a conformity with national goals which contrasts with one's loyalty to God. There is at the heart of the Christian gospel an international dimension. That is presupposed by John's vision in ch. 7. The experience of the Spirit and the product of a hard-won struggle to understand the scope of God's purposes led to an extension of the boundaries of the people of God (see I Cor. 12.13). Nationalism is out of place in the Christian church, even if the contribution to the rich tapestry of the whole needs to be maintained to avoid the emergence of a homogenized and colourless community. After all, the kings of the earth bring *their* gifts to the new Jerusalem (21.24). It was Jesus who, according to the gospels, proclaimed that a national shrine should be internationalized: 'My house shall be a house of prayer for all nations' (Mark 11.17). It is the maintenance of the nation and its interests (which, in reality, means those who have most to gain from the maintenance of those interests) that is frequently going to lead the church to find itself in the position of dissent. There is never going to be a justification for one part of the catholic church taking violent action against another in the name of national sovereignty. History indicates that the preservation of the integrity of a nation is a means of promoting the kind of single-minded devotion that is so roundly condemned in Rev. 13. There can be no circumstances in which the Christian church can give whole-hearted and unqualified support to the nation's enterprises when that means the oppression of others.

COMPROMISE AND CONVICTION

The problem with Revelation is that its language contrasts with the diplomatic niceties of conventional political discourse. It has all the appearance of fanaticism. Dualism of light and darkness, God and Satan, invective against wealth and privilege, resistance against the designs of Satan, all suggest a mindset which offends our sense of decency and our quest for the middle ground (see above, pp. 46ff.). The language of the oppressed, those who, for whatever reason, feel themselves to be on the margins of history, can from the perspective of those who wield power seem hysterical and too apocalyptic in tone. Yet an apocalyptic tone is only just below the surface of most responses when we feel under threat. What Revelation expresses in part is the politics of fear and oppression. As such it is a reflection of *our* innermost fears and most passionate hopes. The book of Revelation expresses those feelings of outrage and stark contrasts in ways which are, however, potentially creative. The tendency to

139

fanaticism, dogmatism and excess is in Revelation channelled into a creative and non-violent trend of activity in which identification with the role of the Lamb is kept at the centre of things. It is assuredly a political response, though the inspiration for it arises from elsewhere than conventional political wisdom.

READING THE SIGNS OF THE TIMES

One of the major challenges posed by Revelation is that it suggests that it is not only legitimate to read the signs of the times, but an essential component of Christian discipleship to do so. The complex task of understanding history from the perspective of God and the gospel has always been fraught with dangers and complications. The temptation to simplicity and the consequent writing off of individuals or societies as enemies of God is all too apparent among those who believe that they have been given divine insight into a situation and can consign people to oblivion with the apparent approval of God. As a reaction against that there has been a long tradition within Christian political theology (due in large part to Augustine) which recognizes God's activity in history but does not allow humans special wisdom in understanding providence.[8] But reading the signs of the times and seeking to understand the political dimension of Christian mission is not to be neglected because of its near impossibility. Revelation emboldens us to practise critical analysis of the state and its demands. That is something which has been taken up with alacrity in the theology of liberation. It is particularly evident in the Kairos Document from South Africa which states that it is a fundamental task of the church's mission to engage in prophetic theology which must involve 'social analysis or what Jesus called reading the signs of the times'.[9] That will demand a wider perspective for those biblical themes like reconciliation, justice and peace than the narrowly individualistic or ecclesiastical focus that Christians have so often given them.

Revelation's hostility to what appeared to be a stable political order and its manifestation of its actual instability are hardly what people who value the maintenance of stability, and the way things are, want to hear. It is quite understandable that those who do not profit from

[8] See R.A. Markus, *Saeculum: History and Society in the Theology of St Augustine*, CUP 1970.
[9] 'The Challenge to the Churches' (the Kairos Document), in *Third World Theology*, Catholic Institute of International Relations 1985, p. 37.

the world as it is find encouragement and solace in Revelation, whereas those who find the world as it is a satisfactory place, and are doing well from it, only desire whatever change is necessary to ensure that this satisfactory state of affairs continues. Christianity has always been suspicious of Mammon because of the desire of those who manage it for stability at any price, for the world as it is rather than what it might become in the kingdom of God. Does that mean that all that can be offered is a critique of capital and the hope that another way might be worked out? The interpretation of Revelation adopted in this commentary has suggested that it does not recommend mere passivity. The scope for creative action in conformity with the gospel may frequently be limited, often undramatic and small-scale. It will be marked by perseverance and faithfulness rather than rapid success. The empowerment of people at the periphery, the Patmos of the present age, may help prevent the emergence of insatiable Babylons, overbearing beasts dazzling with their power and wealth. The critique of human affairs by the weak and marginal may indeed reflect divine wisdom which is frequently vouchsafed to the little people of our world (Matt. 11.25).

Lament for Babylon
18–19.10

This is an amazing chapter. After the graphic vision of Babylon and the brief account of her destruction there is a lament for all that is lost, which asserts the fragility of institutions which are based on anything other than God's righteousness. We are given the impression of the enormous investment which a multitude of people had in her well-being (18.9, 11). The injustice of her activity, however, has been the cause of God's anger against the nations (18.3). Fornication (v. 3, cf. 17.2) speaks about self-gratification which betrays no concern for God's way and as a result ignores the needs of others. It is about short-cuts, thereby ignoring the sensibilities and concerns of others. The accumulation of wealth which this has brought about has come as the result of that kind of process of taking short cuts by means of exploitation. The real character of that process is revealed in 18.13. In the long list of commodities which were part of the trade of Babylon there stand at the end 'slaves and human lives'. A society which ends up making people mere commodities has descended to the religion of the Beast. It was a mark of Rome's might that it grew great as the result of conquest and the exploitation of slave labour[1] in a way reminiscent of Europe in the New World from the sixteenth to the nineteenth centuries. It is a process from which God's people are required to keep their distance (18.4). This sentiment is one that has its echoes elsewhere, e.g. II Cor. 6.14. The command represents a continuing tension for the people of God: is the only way to holiness complete separation, or must it be the case, as Paul suggests in I Cor. 5.9, that there is bound to be a degree of involvement in the old order and no real escape of contamination by it? It is often suggested that as a Christian one's responsibility is to do a job well, whatever it may be, and do it for the glory of God. There are, however, some jobs incompatible with the profession of Christ. Could one be a Christian

[1] See G.E.M. de Ste Croix, *The Class Struggle in the Ancient Greek World from the Archaic Age to the Arab Conquests*, Duckworth 1982.

slave-trader (and owner) for example? The answer of thousands of our predecessors in the faith was a resounding 'yes'. The early church exercised more discrimination over the everyday activities it considered appropriate for its members.

The arrogance of Babylon only compounds the judgement that is coming. There is very little cry for vengeance (though 19.3 comes close to it) despite the persecution described in these chapters ((18.24). It is a celebration of the just and true judgements of God (19.1).

What is remarkable about the description of the destruction of Babylon is that throughout her victims do not exult. The moving lament over the destruction (so poignantly set to music as part of William Walton's *Belshazzar's Feast*) is uttered by those who had done well for themselves as a result of Babylon's power. The rejoicing is left to the heavenly host, which unequivocally rejects Babylon and tells the people of God to come out from her (18.4).

The perspective of the beneficiaries of Babylon's wealth is a remarkably inclusive moment in Revelation. It might raise the question whether John might himself at some stage have been part of the system. Be that as it may, there is some real *sadness* expressed at the passing of the splendour of Babylon. There is no suggestion from the heavenly voices which intersperse the lament, however, that any sorrow should be expressed. But there is a hint of the appreciation of human endeavour, however misguided, which has contributed to Babylon's greatness. We know from the vision of the new Jerusalem that the kings of the earth are mentioned there as bringing their glory into it (21.24). Unlike Babylon (18.2) nothing unclean will ever enter it (21.27). It is not that the glory of the nations is itself a matter for rejection. Its acquisition is the result of deceit (18.23) and at enormous human cost (18.24; 18.13). Babylon is an entirely human creation which, like idols, involves distorted perceptions and unjust acts, and which in its splendour seems invincible (18.10 and 19). It is in reality less than human in its savagery and the defacement of its own dignity and worth in pursuit of its glory (18.23).

The merchants lament that no one any longer trades there (18.11). The list of merchandise is superficially uncontroversial (though the parallels with 9.20 indicate that such items are not morally neutral, but are capable of becoming idols and detracting from true worship). Closer examination reveals that the list of goods in 18.12ff. consists almost entirely of items whose production depends on human labour. There are parallels to John's description of Babylon in

Ezekiel's oracle against Tyre (particularly 27.12ff.). Tyre was a great economic centre. At the very end, John pointedly reminds us that 'human lives' are a commodity too (18.13). It was slave labour along with military conquest which enabled Babylon to become great. The innocent process of buying and selling whose demise is lamented is an exclusive enterprise and intimately bound up with submission to the prevailing culture. We are reminded by John (13.16f.) that only those who are part of the system are allowed to participate. Buying and selling are not innocent enterprises at all, for their conditions are bound up with the whole demonic edifice of that social and economic system. All those commodities are for the benefit of Babylon, the great metropolis and its inhabitants. Goods from the periphery flow thence to the centre. They are produced for the benefit of the powerful who control everything. They are luxuries catering for the opulence of Babylon's élite.

The perspective of those who have profited from Babylon's greatness includes all of us who have become prosperous. We are reminded about the ephemeral nature of that prosperity when viewed from God's perspective (cf. 3.17f.) and the extent to which that prosperity is based on injustice. If *we* identify with the lament of the kings, merchants and sailors, we can truly lament the ease with which the seemingly indestructible and beautiful can be destroyed. We shall mourn our efforts, which we thought were 'public spirited' and the seeming waste of all that talent, time and industry which has gone into making the fabric of society 'great'. But then we shall be reminded of some less palatable facts. A price has had to be paid for the creation of that grand edifice in human labour and life. Equally, we are reminded that to have participated we will have committed 'fornication', abused our human dignity as well as that of others, and above all have ignored our basic obligation to acknowledge our Creator in espousing patterns of behaviour which are unjust.

The way in which John's lament looks at the event from the perspective of the merchants reminds those of us reading this text in the rich world that there is another world whose impoverishment is for our ease and wealth. If we find ourselves identifying with the sorrow of the merchants at the end of civilization, we shall, as Allan Boesak has put it, share 'the viewpoint which is so typically [that] of those who do not known what it means to stand at the bottom of the list'.[2]

---

[2] Allan Boesak, *Comfort and Protest*, pp. 121f.

The judgement of the Word of God
19.11–21

A new dimension to the eschatological process begins. In 4.1 John had seen a door open in heaven. Now heaven opens. It is a decisive moment reminiscent of Mark 1.19 and Acts 10.11, when moments of revelation and insight take place. The open heaven paves the way not for an angelic envoy but for Christ himself (cf. 1.5, 14; 3.7). He possesses that name above every other name (cf. Phil. 2.11; Rev. 2.17). Here the Word of God, incarnate in Jesus, comes to deliver final judgement. It is the culmination of a process started in the life of Jesus, for, as the Gospel of John indicates, the tabernacling of the divine Word brings judgement to the world in the career of Jesus (John 3.16ff.). He comes on the scene as the leader of a body (apparently) of martyrs ready for the eschatological banquet (19.14, cf. 19.8). The ensuing struggle is not with conventional weapons of war. It is the words which judge (cf. Isa. 11.4 and IV Ezra 13). It is the words of the Messiah that will endure for ever (Mark 13.31), and which will condemn those who oppose the righteousness of God. He is revealed to the world now as what he really is, what he is already recognized as in heaven (Rev. 5.9). Now he is manifest to the whole of creation (cf. 1.19); he is king of kings (cf. 17.14).

This powerful description indicates that judgement is not merely an individual matter: God's concern is for the establishment of right in human affairs. Also, the presentation of Christ as judge is one which manifests some of those basic characteristics of the gospel. He comes with garments dipped in blood, *his own* blood shed on the cross. Above all, it is a reminder that followers of Jesus will not be fatalistic about the present state of affairs and imagine that the God they worship can allow the injustices of human history to remain for ever. We may prefer a God who will treat the rich and powerful in the same way as the humble and meek, as if their way of life was of no concern to God. Revelation reminds us that this cannot be the case. If our view of God is comfortable, and merely supportive to our prejudices and desires, then we may be guilty of idolatry. The challenging picture of Christ as judge is iconoclastic and disturbing.

In 19.17ff. the judgement is presented as a *fait accompli*. There is little attempt to satisfy the curiosity about how it will be done. The list of those judged in v. 18 is consistent with the perspective of the book in which those who maintain and benefit from the *status quo* are under particular condemnation. While the 'small' can be expected to be led astray as they desperately seek for their own survival (13.16), it is kings, captains and the mighty who are prominently mentioned (cf. 6.15). Already in 17.12 mention has been made of the opposition of the Beast to the Lamb. The Beast and false prophet are cast into the lake of fire and the rest slain with the sword from Christ's mouth (19.21; cf. II Thess. 2.8).

The pattern of justice and judgement is gruesome in its execution (19.21b). In a world where force and violence are recognized as the only credible method of dealing with problems, the words that proceed from the mouth of the Messiah are seen to be devastating (cf. II Thess. 2.8; cf. Isa. 11.4). That reminds us of something that our all too easy use of words disguises from us: their creative and destructive power (cf. Gen. 1.3; Ps. 33.6, 9). Words can torment hearers as much as the eschatological judgement itself (11.6). In our pursuit of the better way it is surely our task to explore patterns of challenge which seek to conform to God's way without being either destructive or merely pusillanimous.[1] It is Jesus' words recalled by the Spirit which assist in the conviction of the world of sin, righteousness and judgement (John 16.8ff.) and are the cornerstone of the indictment against a world that prefers darkness to light.

However awesome these images are, we are not allowed to get involved in speculation about what the future will be like. The description of judgement is economical in the extreme. Only what is necessary to make the point about the message of justice and judgement and the significance of present words and deeds is included. To this extent Revelation differs little from the Gospels of John and Matthew in placing all the emphasis on present decisions, attitudes and conduct (John 5.24f.; Matt. 25.31ff.)

---

[1] See e.g. W. Wink, *Engaging the Powers: Discernment and Resistance in a World of Domination*, Fortress Press 1992.

The triumph of righteousness
20

This passage has not received the attention it deserves. It looks forward to a period when the messianic reign will take place *on earth*. It is a fufilment then of the prayer of Jesus: 'thy kingdom come, thy will be done on earth as it is in heaven', which forms such a central part of our worship. Within Christianity, however, it has become such a commonplace to suppose that the destiny of the blessed is heaven, to be with God, that it comes as something of a surprise to note that for much of the first hundred or so years of the church's life virtually all Christians looked forward to the coming of the reign of the Messiah on earth. This passage is only unusual in giving it a specific length (20.3). In all other respects it represents what most of our ancestors in the faith who wrote the New Testament looked forward to, as did contemporary Jewish writers. It only disappears from mainstream Christian thinking much later, when Augustine finally set the seal on the repudiation of a this-worldly kingdom in his *City of God*.[1]

There are curious features about these final chapters which have led commentators to wonder whether there is a juxtaposition of different sources in chs.19–21. There appear to be two judgements (19.11ff. and 20.7ff.) and two descriptions of the new age (20.4 and 21.1ff.). Such repetitions are found elsewhere in Revelation as we have noted. In chs. 7 and 14 we have anticipations of the echatological gathering of the people of God. In both cases their inclusion can be understood in the light of the particular contrasts made between threat and promise at these particular junctures in the text. The juxtaposition of a messianic reign of a thousand years and a new creation is not without parallel in contemporary Jewish sources. In IV Ezra 7 and Syr. Baruch 25ff., both written a little later than Revelation, we have a similar sequence, though there is no mention in either text of the messianic reign lasting a thousand years (it is

[1] See further B.E. Daley, *The Hope of the Early Church: a Handbook of Patristic Eschatology*, CUP 1991.

four hundred in IV Ezra 7.28). Its presence in both these texts suggests the central role that a this-worldly vindication of the divine promises played. This repetition is understandable if we give full weight to John's *vision*. The logic of the structured argument is not that of the apocalyptic vision. Attributing traditions to different sources may satisfy our desire to make a text conform to certain literary canons. The text as it stands is not nonsense, nor is it impossible to expound the contrasting climaxes to the story of salvation in these chapters.

Belief in the millennium deserves much greater prominence than it has had. At the centre of our faith is the confession that Jesus is raised from the dead. Resurrection from the dead is after all the transformation of that destined to death to share the life of a renewed world. Salvation does not involve an escape into a world beyond. We do not in our creeds confess our belief in the immortality of the soul but of resurrection from the dead. The hope for a thousand-year reign of the Messiah on earth is entirely consistent with that hope. The inspiration for the pattern of human existence which led to the death, destruction, oppression and other acts described in the previous chapters will be absent (20.2). Satan will be bound, and so deceit and confusion will no longer lead the nations astray. Those who reign have shown themselves fit to do so because they are the ones who have identified themselves with the way of the Lamb even at the cost of their lives (21.4). They are to be priests, the calling of the whole people of God (1.6; 5.10, cf. I Peter 2.9). They are peculiarly qualified because of their espousal of another form of governance to exercise an intermediary role. It is those whose life follows in the footsteps of the Messiah by refusing to accept the injustice of the old order and holding out for something different who can truly represent humanity to God and God to humanity. It is an age which will be marked by that alternative pattern of life which had been followed by a minority and ridiculed in the old order. It is now *seen* to be relevant and applicable. It is what millions have dreamed of and longed for. Some sought to translate it into action, thereby offering glimpses of it in the difficult circumstances of an unjust order. Frequently they may have failed, but underlying it all was the conviction that something better for every man, woman, child and creature must be possible. The messianic kingdom can outlast the greatest forces hurled against it. Its force is enough to destroy all that stands against it because it has its origins in God's righteousness (20.9).

The messianic reign is dependent on the restraint of Satan. We have described here the earthly parallel to what is set out in 12.7ff. There is in that context no longer an accuser of the brethren in the heavenly court (12.10). Their access to God is no longer threatened. Here the deceiving of all people and the distortion of minds and lives takes place no longer (cf. 12.9; 13.14), thus enabling a proper sense of justice and responsibility. The contrast between the binding and loosing of Satan (20.2 and 7) indicates the extent to which that supra-individual web of deceit enslaves humanity. The restraint of Satan means the messianic reign; the loosing of Satan leads to deceit and rebellion once more against God and the Lamb. Jesus promised the disciples the power to do *exactly* what the angel with the key to the abyss could do: the power to bind and loose (Matt. 16.19; 18.18; John 20.23). It is their privilege to be involved in that superhuman struggle in the old age. Faith in the Messiah means the power to build foundations of a community against which the gates of hell can never prevail, though it is easy to let Satan loose and to cause 'scandal' by looking at things from a human rather than a divine perspective (Matt. 16.23).

The binding of Satan is reminiscent of the binding of Legion in Mark 5.3 (cf. Isa. 65.4) and earlier in Mark 3.22ff. In the parable in Mark 3.27, Jesus had talked of binding the strong man and then plundering his house. The binding of Satan takes place in Mark 5.1ff. when Legion is cast out and into the herd of pigs which rushes down into the sea, thus enabling the man who had spent his time in the mountains among the tombs, cutting himself, to sit clothed and in his right mind. The elect are sitting with Jesus (20.4, cf. 3.21) clothed with white robes (3.18). That is the lot of those who have resisted Satan even at the cost of their lives (20.4, cf. 12.11).

Commentators have pointed to the Roman military imagery used of the demons in Mark 5.[2] It is the Roman impostors and institutions which are singled out for mention in 19.19f. Connections between the two receive support if we look at the Lucan version of the story. Whereas Mark talks of the sea as the destination of the demons (5.13), Luke's version of the story uses the same word as Revelation (8.32, cf. Rev. 19.20; 20.14). In Luke 8.31 Luke uses the word 'abyss', a word used in Rev. 9.1, 11; 11.7; 17.8; 20.3, in some of which passages there is close connection with the Beast. Such links are a pointed reminder of the cosmic struggle against the powers

---

[2] See e.g. Wengst, *Pax Romana and the Peace of Jesus Christ*, pp. 65f.

of this age and the evil they embody already at work in Jesus' ministry.

When read in the light of the book of Revelation, this powerful and complex story exhibits the superhuman struggle which lies just below the surface of Jesus' engagement with individuals and institutions. In an area of uncleanness, where pigs were tended, Jesus came and challenged the spirit of Legion. Why Legion? The links with the military forces of the Roman occupying power is no coincidence. The man embodied the dislocation of life and hope caused by the military presence. As with many sensitive souls throughout the ages, the disintegration of his life was a sign of the disintegration of the world. He embodied in himself the fragmentation of existence and acted as a scapegoat for the evil pressures and powers which dislocated the world and the life and land of the people of God. That same sensitivity enabled him to recognize who Jesus was and to see the upheaval that the Son of God was to bring to his own life and people. The destruction of Legion took place when the unclean spirits entered the swine and perished in the sea. It is not too difficult to make a link with the imagery of the book of Revelation, where the judgement on the unjust powers and institutions, before the reign of God can finally come, involves their end in the lake of fire (Rev. 19.20). The integration of the individual in the gospel story is a proleptic glimpse of that harmony which will come in the millennium, when fragmented lives have been restored and the disorder which masquerades as peace has been overcome.

That link between Revelation and the gospels is evident elsewhere. There are contacts between Luke's Gospel and Revelation in addition to those already noted. Several of these are apparent in Luke's version of the eschatological discourse (Luke 21). The features are distinctive and suggest that Luke has a broader horizon to the prophecy, more in keeping with that found in Revelation. Thus in Luke 21.28 the reference to liberation suggests that more could have been said, but there has instead been concentration on the time of distress preceding it (Luke 21.23, cf. I Cor. 7.26 and 28). What Luke predicts are days of vengeance (picking up on Isa. 61.2 but omitted in the quotation of these verses in Luke 4.19). The tribulation in 21.25 reminds us of the chaos in Rev. 6.8f., as also does the reaction of humanity in 21.26 (cf. Rev. 6.15ff.) in the face of the time of wrath (21.26, cf. Rev. 6.16). The allusive reference to the trampling of Jerusalem by Gentiles (21.24) recalls John's vision in Rev. 11.1ff. Elsewhere in the story of Jesus, it is Luke who reports the absence of Satan from the life of Jesus (Luke 4.21; cf. 22.3 and 7.22; cf. Rev. 20.2ff.). It is the Gospel of Luke which portrays Jesus as offering an interpretation of the mission of the seventy and their triumph over the power of darkness which is linked with the vision of Satan's fall from heaven (Luke 10.18, cf. Rev. 12.7ff.). The critical moment of Jesus' death is marked by an eclipse (there is an explicit reference in 23.45, cf. Rev. 8.12 and 16.10). Such links are all the more significant, as Luke's Gospel is widely assumed to reflect a diminution of interest in things eschatological and apocalyptic in the face of disappointment over the delay of Christ's coming in glory. This (by no means exhaustive) collection of references suggests, on the contrary, the need of an evangelist to tell the story of Jesus in such a way that even by subtle hints its apocalyptic dimension could be brought out. It is as if the full significance of the story cannot be told without resort to the more profound insight which apocalyptic language offers.

The destruction of Satan and his host comes not by any battle. Fire descends from heaven (20.9, cf. II Kings 1.10, 12; Luke 9.54; II Thess. 2.8). It is a deliverance reminiscent of old, particularly the deliverance of Zion from foreign invaders (Isa. 38ff., cf. Pss. 46; 78.68; 87.2). In the various accounts of judgement there is concentration on the institutional manifestation of evil: the Beast and Babylon. In the second judgement the focus is on the root of all evil, Satan who deceives the world and persuades a messianically ordered universe to oppose God and God's elect (20.8).

Christ offers a way to bring order to the chaos; Satan the contrary: the distortion of reality, the false sense of security, power and the life which conforms to its surroundings and never challenges its assumptions. It is that which stands in the way of the perception of and response to the divine justice. Acceptance of the Beast and committing 'fornication' with Babylon are worship of Satan, and involve being marked with its character manifested in the stamp of the Beast. Subservience to the Beast may bring short-term relief, but is eternally corrupting. Satan's agents, particularly the state and its institutions can claim universal rule and adoration (13.4) and even appear to be Christlike (13.3). Such a model is based on deceit (12.9) and involves the persecution of those who do God's work of justice, peace and reconciliation (20.9, cf. 12.13).

The judgement itself is an interlocking process of consultation of two books (cf. Daniel 7.10). This might at first sight suggest a deterministic view of salvation where election depends on whether one's name has been included by God in the book or not. The Lamb's book of life is intimately linked with refusal to compromise with the Beast and Babylon (13.8). 3.5 suggests that inclusion in the book is not inevitable. The twofold emphasis on judgement according to works (20.12, 13) is consistent with the rest of the book which is intended to encourage repentance by the believer (chs. 2–3) and non-believer alike (9.20). That is what we would expect from the thrust of the Matthean Jesus' proclamation (Matt. 7.21 and 25.31ff.).

A new heaven and a new earth
21.1–22.5

In a real sense this chapter marks the climax of the whole book. In it we find the culmination and fulfilment of the process that had begun in ch. 5 with the Lamb receiving the sealed scroll. The vision of God's tabernacling with humanity marks the climax of the eschatological drama.

In Rev. 4 the seer is granted a glimpse into the environs of God. Here God the Creator and Liberator is acknowledged, and, as we notice from ch. 5, it is from the God of the universe that the historical process begins which leads to the establishment of a new aeon. In the following chapters we find the picture of a world afflicted but unrepentant. Indeed, it manifests precisely the kind of misguided devotion to evil which is shown up in all its horror in the light of the life and death of Christ and has to be rooted out before God's kingdom can finally come. In Rev. 4ff. God is still in heaven, and it is there that the heavenly host sing his praise and magnify his name. Compare that with Rev. 21, where God's dwelling is on earth; it is no longer in heaven.

HEAVEN: God surrounded by those who do God's will

EARTH: Humankind unwilling to do God's will

HEAVEN
ON EARTH

Rev. 4–20   Rev. 21–22

The contrast between heaven and earth disappears in the new creation. Now the tabernacle of God is with men and women (7.9ff. suggests that the new Jerusalem is not reserved solely for the male celibates of 14.4), and they will be God's people (21.3). God's dwelling is not to be found above the cherubim in heaven; for the throne is set right in the midst of the new Jerusalem, where the living waters stream from the throne of God (22.1). God's servants marked with the divine name will see God face to face (22.4). It is only in the new creation that there will be the conditions for God and humanity to dwell in that harmony which was impossible while there was rejection of the divine righteousness in human affairs. Heaven on earth is the fulfilment of God's purposes. God is no longer apparently far off but immediate and manifest – very much part of that world of perfection and evident in it as God was in Paradise (Gen. 3.8). Indeed, the inhabitants will be God's children and carry the divine name on their heads: they will be identified with the character of God and enjoy the divine presence unmediated. But, as Paul reminds us in II Cor. 5.17, that new creation is not merely something to look forward to. In Christ already there is the possibility in the power of God's Spirit of bringing about that new creation in individual lives and corporate action.

Rekindling the prophetic hopes of a new beginning (Isa. 42.9), God speaks directly on one of the few occasions in the Apocalypse (cf. 18.5): 'Now God has his dwelling with humanity' (21.3). It is appropriate that, now the barrier between God and the world has been destroyed, God's will can be manifested directly. At the moment of triumph of divine righteousness the needy are remembered ('To the thirsty I will give water from the spring as a gift' 21.6, cf. Matt. 5.6). Just as the Spirit enabled those who accepted the Messiah, the Son of God, in the midst of the old order to be sons and daughters of God (Gal. 4.6), so now that promise is fulfilled. All who bel the new age and own its values, whether now or in the future, are God's children. The promise to David is extended to the whole people (II Sam. 7.14). Twice there is a list of those excluded from the new Jerusalem (21.8, 27; 22.15). They are the ones who by their deeds behave in the same way as the whore of Babylon. By their acts they show that they believe they can take short cuts to satisfy their desires, or in their practice of righteousness, or by sorcery hope to be able to manipulate God. In the midst of the glory and perfection, the references to those excluded sound a jarring note. Even here the reader is shocked out of complacency by the reality of imperfection at the doors of the new Jerusalem.

The contrast between the new Jerusalem and Babylon is stark. In 17.3 John is in the Spirit and taken to a desert place, whereas in 21.10 he is taken to a high mountain. In ch. 21 he sees a bride prepared for her husband; in ch. 17 a great harlot. In both cases John's guide is one of the angels of the seven bowls (17.1, cf. 21.9). Whereas Babylon (17.5) is seated on many waters supported by the Beast, the new Jerusalem comes down out of heaven (21.1). Some of the jewels used in the construction of the new Jerusalem in 21.19 appear also in the description of Babylon in 17.4, and of her trade in 18.11, once again suggesting the proximity of the misguided and unjust human projects to God's own. Jerusalem's construction is like the very appearance of God (Rev. 4.3). Its gates are made of pearl, a gem found naturally, not the creation of human hands (cf. II Cor. 5.1ff.).

The lengthy description of the city shows that it is represented as based on the plan of the tabernacle (21.16, cf. I Kings 6.19), thus extending the realm of the holy to the environs of the whole city. The symmetrical character of the city speaks of perfection. Yet it is perfection rooted at least in part in human endeavour: on its twelve foundations are the names of the twelve apostles (cf. Eph. 2.20). Those vacillating faint-hearts of the gospels turn out to be founda-tions of the new Jerusalem. Surely here there is encouragement for those daunted by the task of following the Messiah. What is more, there is offered the possibility of *contributing* to the building of the new Jerusalem. That is not confined to apostles only. Those who conquer (15.2) will have the right to become pillars in the temple, just as Peter was a pillar (3.12, cf. Gal. 2.9; I Tim. 3.15).

There has been much discussion over the extent to which human endeavour could contribute to the new age. For Paul in I Cor. 3.10ff. there is no other foundation than Jesus Christ. Indeed, Paul con-trasts the lasting building with those that do not endure. It is possible that Paul may hint at some of the ingredients of the building of the city of the new age, mentioned in 21.18f., when he speaks of gold, precious stones (silver is mentioned by Paul but is only a product of Babylon in Revelation). Nevertheless Paul sets himself up as one who by God's grace is a wise builder who lays the true foundation. In other words, the construction of the eschatological community, the new Jerusalem based on Jesus Christ, is an activity started *here and now*. In all these passages we have some support for our modern notions of 'building the kingdom'. It is not all left to some eschatological miracle; human agents infused with the Spirit of the new age may contribute to that future reign of God here and now in the midst of the debris of the old order.

There is no temple because the whole of the city is a holy place, and God does not need to be confined to a holy space in the new Jerusalem. This contrasts with 7.15, where reference is made to serving God in the temple (that phrase is repeated in 22.3 but without reference to the temple). That understanding of holiness which sought to establish it in the midst of the world and in the lives of people of flesh and blood is echoed elsewhere in the New

155

Testament (e.g. I Cor. 3.16; 6.19; cf. II Cor. 6.16). A renewed temple
is often included in eschatological passages in contemporary Jewish
writings, so its explicit omission here deserves to be noted. There
was ambivalence, even hostility, towards the temple in early Christianity (Acts 6.7; cf. Mark 14.58 and John 4.25). Like the Pharisees,
the first Christians had a view of holiness rooted in practical living in
the midst of the variety of human community. The imagery in
Revelation owes much to Ezek. 40ff. and also the later chapters of
Isaiah (e.g. Rev. 21.22f., cf. Isa. 60.1, 3, 5 etc.). This last is a section
where contemporary temple worship is viewed with some disap-
proval (Isa. 66.1ff., cf. 56.7).

The temple is no permanent part of the biblical story. The divine
provision for liturgy in the Torah centres on the tabernacle. The
erection of the temple, though in the narrative of Israel's history it is
sanctioned by God, is intimately linked with the establishment of
kingship and a royal dynasty, institutions fraught with danger and
the risk of decline from the standards of holiness expected by God
(e.g. I Sam. 8 and 10, cf. Deut. 17.14ff.). The lack of a divine sanction
for the temple in the Torah is more than made up in later Jewish
literature. Thus one of the Dead Sea Scrolls, the Temple Scroll from
Cave 11,[1] has the plan of temple and city revealed to Moses, thus
giving it that divine sanction denied in the Torah itself.

We cannot easily gloss over the clear conviction expressed in
I Sam. 7 and I Kings 5 and 8 that it was as a fulfilment of God's will
that the temple was built by Solomon to be a dwelling-place for the
Most High (Ps. 46.4). Nevertheless that temple was destroyed after
the invasion of Nebuchadnezzar. That may have seemed to be the
mark of (ultimate) judgement. In the light of that, the justification for
the rebuilding of the temple must have been questioned. Indeed,
the codification of liturgical law which reached its final stages in
the exile in the aftermath of the destruction looks back to the
movable tabernacle in the time before the temple, not the static building in Zion. There was a concerted campaign backed by appeal to
divine authority, in the prophecy of Haggai especially, to restore the
temple. The argument of Haggai's prophecy is that the impoverishment of Israel is the result of the neglect of 'old-fashioned' temple
religion. If only the temple is rebuilt (and scarce resources thereby
diverted to the restoration of cultic activity and the particular inter-

---

[1] See *The Temple Scroll: an Introduction, Translation and Commentary* by J. Maier, ET
(JSOT Supplement Series 34), Sheffield 1985.

ests, both social and economic, of the priestly caste), then all would be well in the land (Haggai 1.4ff.).

Such arguments are familiar to religious people down the ages. A focus of religious life in a building has enormous attractions as a way of dealing with human need for reassurance. It is likely that there were those in Haggai's day who resisted the restoration of the temple (Isa. 66.1ff.) and the narrowness of vision that it involved, especially when it meant denial of the justice of God and the true mission of Israel to bring that justice to the nations (Isa. 49). We cannot be sure, but possibly some leading New Testament figures (Jesus, Stephen, the author of the Gospel of John, Hebrews and John of Patmos) may have stood in this latter tradition.

This tradition raises an important question about the enormous investment of the Christian church down the centuries in its buildings. Revelation evokes a most physical structure for the eschatological space, yet is clear about the face to face relationship between God and humanity at the centre of its life (22.4f.). The temple is superfluous. Yet a special space or place has become central to our understanding of religion. Our need to create holy spaces resembles Peter's desire on the mount of Transfiguration to build tabernacles to preserve the divine (Luke 9.5 and parallels). He failed to understand that the holy space was the body of a crucified man (Mark 15.38) and a group of people who identified with him (Matt. 18.20; I Cor. 12). It was not in the midst of a city or religious enclave that the focus of the holy was to be found: 'Jesus ... suffered outside the gate. Let us then go to him outside the camp, bearing the stigma that he bore' (Heb. 13.12f.). What is most apparent in Revelation is that the presence of divine holiness and the testimony to the divine purposes are in no way dependent on buildings, but on the maintenance of human community where God in Christ is acknowledged, and an alternative vision of reality maintained and celebrated. The hope and commitment to the crucified Messiah which is folly to humanity (I Cor. 3.19) do not depend at all on a building, but on the creation of a holy people where God's Spirit can dwell and an alternative vision and practice can be preserved. It is in that sharing and engagement that there can be glimpsed something of the life in the new Jerusalem.

It is apparent that within certain confines this is not an exclusive vision. The light of God's glory is a light for the nations (Isa. 60) and the glory of the old age is to be brought in. It is those who ignored God by raising the material to the level of God and their own self-interest above God's justice who are excluded (21.27). Those whose names are written in the book of life are explicitly linked with those who have not compromised or collaborated with the old order (13.8). It is worth noting that at the head of the list of those excluded from the new Jerusalem are the cowards (21.8) who refused to stand up and be counted when protest against injustice was needed. In 21.8 (cf. 22.15) those who were infected with the sorcery of Babylon, the deceit of wealth and the temptations that trade produced, are also excluded.

John's vision is of a city. It is therefore communal rather than individual, a reminder that biblical practice and hope is centred from first to last on relationships between humanity and God and with one another. Christianity has in its history focussed so often on hope for the individual that it has lost sight of the central place community plays in past, present and future expressions of human destiny. As we grow ever more concerned about life in our cities and thousands seek escape in some rural idyll, it is a salutary reminder that the fulfilment of God's purposes is centred on a city, in a community which reflects the situation of paradise (22.1f., cf. Gen. 2.10). This is God's paradise. It is different from the presumption of the earthly city in believing that wealth could make paradise (cf. Ezek. 28.12ff.). That travesty led to the exploitation of human lives as a pseudo-paradise was created for a few.

In a startling link with Ezek. 47.1, images of paradise and city come together (22.1, cf. Gen. 2.9f.). The climax of John's vision is to see the throne of God now shared by the Lamb (cf. 7.15). That throne which had hitherto been in heaven becomes the focal point of the new Jerusalem. In so doing it is itself transformed. Whereas in the Jewish tradition on which John's vision depends (Dan. 7.9f., cf. I Enoch 14.20ff.) there flowed from the throne a river of fire threatening all who drew near it (a point made in Rev. 15 where the sea of glass mingled with fire seems to mark an enormous obstacle), that threat has now disappeared. A river of fire is replaced by the water of life; the sea is no more (21.1). There is only life-giving water (cf. John 7.38). In contrast to the destruction of nature and humanity with which so many of the middle chapters of the apocalypse are marked, we now have a tree bearing fruit which is for the healing of the nations. Of course, this offer has been there all the time. In the old age the offer of healing has been rooted in the recognition of injustice and the need for repentance and the acceptance of the way of the Lamb. Self-awareness, understanding and faithful following of the Lamb wherever it goes are what lead to healing and wholeness.

The climax of the description of the new age in 22.4 has the inhabitants sharing God's character (cf. in other terminology Phil. 3.20 and I John 3.2) and seeing God face to face (cf. Matt. 5.8). Moses was unable to see God, for no one can see God and live (Ex. 33.20). That beatific vision in the old age was focussed in Christ (John 14.9, cf. 1.18). It is now offered to all because God will be all in all (I Cor. 15.28, cf. II Peter 1.4). In that situation all will share in the reign of God on earth (22.5) fulfilling all the promises made in 1.6; 5.10 (cf. Matt. 19.28). That reign is rooted in a redefined concept of kingship (5.5). Jesus made a contrast with the practices of kings in Mark 10.42. Also in his dialogue with Pilate, Jesus represents a portrait of kingship which is not 'of this world' (John 18.36). That involves no denial of power but means the offering of ways of using that power which are participative, humane and non-exploitative. The beatific vision marks the climax of life in the new Jerusalem. Yet it is not merely something to be looked forward to in this life and only experienced after death. Jesus reminded his disciples that the one who sits on the throne of glory is to be seen in the midst of the injustice of the old order. Ignored by most, the hungry, the thirsty, the strangers, the naked and the ill offer, paradoxically, a present glimpse of the beatific vision (Matt. 25.31ff.). The appropriate response is not to indulge in the quest for glory but to minister to the needy. In so doing those who do so will be surprised that they have already seen the Lord face to face and shared the glory of the new Jerusalem.

Take these words to heart!
22.6–21

The conclusions of the book return to some of the hortatory themes of the letters to the seven churches. We are left in no doubt about the importance that John thought should be attached to his book. They are words of prophecy (22.7) and should never be tampered with (22.18). The words of the book like their author, Jesus, are faithful and true (19.11). There is need to *keep* the words of prophecy, not only in the sense of preserving but in *practice* too (cf. 12.17; 14.12). John tells his readers that they should be treated with the same kind of authority as the words of the Old Testament (cf. Deut. 4.2). It is a curious fact that the book in the New Testament with the most exalted claim to authority (a point quoted by Martin Luther, see above, pp. 26 f.) is the one that is least read or understood and most widely despised. Yet it is a Revelation from Jesus Christ (1.1). Even if we cannot understand it in its entirety and are uncomfortable with the import of its message we need to be able to offer ourselves convincing reasons for ignoring it. It not only stands at the end of the New Testament but also at the end of the Christian Bible. Arguably it may offer us the key to understand the whole story, because it points forward to the fulfilment of God's purposes of which all else give only a partial and fragmentary example. We have seen that its message is about God and human history. Its scope is panoramic and its focus on Jesus as the key to understanding the fulfilment of God's justice central. Its different style and language suggest that the perspective of God's reign demands new ways of explaining and understanding as well as acting.

John's role is important, as has been stressed earlier (10.11). He is not to suppose that angels are superior to him (22.9), for John is a prophet. In Revelation we are in a confused world of angels and humans. John's role is to act as God's scribe to the angels of the churches. He too has an angelic task (22.16, cf. Mal. 3.1, where the prophet is called an 'angel', just as John the Baptist was in Mark 1.3, cf. Ex. 23.20).

There is a yearning for the coming of Jesus (22.17 and 20). That coming is one that is longed for to bring justice, but it is like the Day of the Lord (Amos 5.18ff.), a day of darkness for those who are unjust. The coming of Christ is not just future but, as 3.20 reminds us, a present and threatening parousia for a self-deceiving, complacent church and world.

With care Revelation can enable us to look back over the biblical story and make sense of the diverse parts of which scripture is made up. In addition, it pointedly reminds us of the demands made on us in our historical circumstances by a God who regards every action as of significance . Here we can begin to glimpse what the Spirit says to the churches and learn to respond accordingly: 'Happy are those wash their robes clean' (22.14, cf. 7.14). That can mean nothing else than identification with the Messiah who offered 'an even better way' (I Cor.13.1).

There will always be human spirits who will not resign themselves to cynicism ... who will not join the ranks of those who trust only in the order and power of the strongest. Like Jesus they will dream of a world for all and accept the risks entailed in establishing it. And they will continue to be condemned and crucified for this hope of theirs ... The question of all of the martyrs rises as a cry to God: How long, O Lord , how long? And the Lord, who is merciful, resurrects our hope, transforming the question into a plea: Thy kingdom ... on earth as it is in heaven.[1]

---

[1] Leonardo Boff, *Way of the Cross, Way of Justice*, pp. 107f.

EPILOGUE

What are we to make of this outburst of visionary emotion and hope?
Are we not left wondering whether this is not the crazed musing of
an unhinged mind which has nothing whatsoever to contribute to
the understanding of our world or our future? Questions like this
actually go to the heart of the Christian religion. If the horizon of
hope is removed from it, it becomes a mere torso of a cluster of ideas
and practices which confront us in the Bible. Christianity's rejection
of the detail of the Jewish law is based on the fulfilment of hope, and
its outlook totally determined by its messianism and the conviction
that we live 'between the times' of Christ's incarnation and parousia.
If that overall structure of belief and practice is removed, there is not
much left, and precious little that is distinctive. Revelation reminds
us as forcibly as any New Testament writing: to deny hope is to take
away Christianity's heart.

Revelation reminds us of this hope in such a world-shattering and
mind-blowing way that the question of the extent to which hope and
reality coincide becomes more acute. How can we believe any of this
when this age did not come to an end within the short time that John
expected? Doesn't this undermine the validity of the whole? Such
questions are not susceptible of easy answers. Our fears about the
environment (and in the past decade or so about the possibility of
nuclear catastrophe) have enabled us to get more in touch with the
apocalyptic outlook. It is much more difficult to contemplate the
hope for a world where 'sorrow and sighing will flee away'. We
recognize the deep-rooted sinfulness of societies and social structures and our often fatalistic acceptance of there being no alternative.
In such a situation the language of Revelation gives voice to our fears
and our hopes.

Are we to see these sentiments merely as a moral imperative
spurring us to greater endeavours on behalf of those in need? Or is
there something more than that? The account we give of ourselves as
Christians is rooted in the extraordinary story of the Messiah who

162

was executed, of hopes dashed and restored, of ourselves as a community grounded in hope and living, however tentatively, in anticipation of the fulfilment of hope. That is a vulnerable place to be when we live in the midst of so much despair, so much that contradicts what we understand to be the way of Christ. An account of ourselves must assert that however fragmented our meeting to break bread may be, however tentative our witness, our convictions that things will be different, our attempts to do things differently *are* connected intimately with that better world still to come. Revelation speaks not merely of an ideal to be striven for but of a reality that infuses all thought and practice.

Revelation points forward and makes us look again at our present way of viewing things. It demands of us a readiness to break with ways of thinking which are hemmed in by our poverty of vision. Instead of viewing things from the perspective of the old order we are asked (indeed, compelled by the Spirit) to look at things afresh with minds being transformed by the eschatological realities unseen but real. At various times and places we can do that without ever fully understanding how things will be (I John 3.2). We groan and travail with the rest of creation in a mixture of fear, uncertainty and longing. As we wait for a birth, we do not know what the child will be like and yet there is a process linking the travail and the moment of birth. It is that process with regard to our hope that Revelation brings most forcibly to our attention and which New Testament language about the resurrection emphasizes. The resurrection is a symbol of hope and a sign of the contradiction of our faith. Whatever may have happened (and the New Testament accounts have the capacity to make seem ordinary that which quite clearly is extraordinary) we are confronted in the resurrection of Jesus with a symbol which parallels the tangled hope of Revelation. In it the complex strands of hope are to some extent unravelled and the colour and intricacy of the story of which we are a part examined.

We are thereby emboldened to hope. We are not condemned to grey realism for ever. That is both encouraging and embarrassing. We would prefer to think like everyone else. We would like to be thought commonsensical, yet at every turn Revelation seems to condemn us to be written off as dreamers at best or fanatics at worst. As Paul found too, looking at things differently is not without its problems (I Cor. 3.19). There is no virtue in irrationality, silliness or the refuge of a fantasy world. It is our responsibility to think clearly and carefully, but with our thinking informed by that disturbing

163

story of Jesus and its culmination, only glimpses of which we can now see. The visions of Revelation do not provide the currency of our everyday exchange of ideas and patterns of existence. Dreams are important for us, but to allow them to determine our every step, and suppose that the detail is in some sense *as it stands* prescriptive, is to fall into the trap of literalism. To ignore our dreams is to ignore the possibility of understanding ourselves better. That is true of apocalyptic dreams. We are not supposed to act them out as if the chaos of our subconscious necessarily offers the blue-print for life. Apocalyptic offers us no excuse for resort to fantasy, particularly of a literalist kind. The purpose of it all is understanding leading to more informed and obedient lives. As Revelation itself indicates, that is manifested in very practical matters which may be controversial, costly to ourselves and our public esteem, and above all will refuse to conform to the expectations of society as it is unless those demands are compatible with Christ.

Probably we shall only infrequently find ourselves in that position of being part of a wider movement for change which will bring about a programme of justice on a large scale. More often it will all be very small fare and hardly the fulfilment of the vision of hope set out in the pages of Revelation. Yet we need to recall that what we do here and now is bound up with that fulfilment. The pattern of discipleship is not one that inflicts its values on others. Its mission is to persevere and by example and good works persuade others while accepting that the action may at times provoke hostility rather than acceptance. This practice, non-violent in outlook and determined in its non-conformity and attention to everyday detail, is the necessary expense of those who have caught a sight of that vision which Revelation offers. They may be non-conformists, but non-conformity does not demand prickliness or defensiveness. Like the Lamb, the disciples will be vulnerable and open, often feeling defenceless in conventional terms and with little to offer by way of a clever riposte. Their security is rooted in the ultimate conviction that they are worthy in God's eyes.

We dare to hope not merely because of some psychological need or the powerlessness which comes from inability to change our circumstances to our liking. Our hope is rooted in the story we tell of ourselves and our God and the sense we make of our world in the light of it. It is not merely our story we proclaim, nor even the church's, but God's. As we tell the story, we cannot but hope and pray that God's kingdom will come on earth as it already is in heaven. As we break bread together we echo the words of the former head of the Jesuit order, Pedro Aruppe, who said that as long as there is any one in the world who is hungry, our eucharist is incomplete. Revelation has nothing as explicit as Matt. 25.31ff. in challenging us to respond to Christ in the needy. Nevertheless in outlining the hope in Rev. 7.16 and 21.6, the expectation is that those needs will be met. Ignoring those needs and explaining faithfulness to Jesus without attention to them or to our hope is to undermine the claim of our worship of God. We run the risk of leaving Christ knocking outside the door of our churches in the persons of the poor and outcast while imagining that the Lord is here. It is because of Jesus that we hope for something different and dare to warn of the effects of ignoring God's justice. It is because of our hope that we look to our own practice and seek at every opportunity to embody the promptings of the eschatological spirit in words and deeds. These must mirror that time when sorrow and sighing will flee away and each human will be recognized, equally stamped with the name of our God; then we shall see God face to face:

Vulnerable God,
> you challenge the powers that rule this world
> through the needy, the compassionate,
> and those who are filled with longing.
> Make us hunger and thirst to see right prevail,
> and single-minded in seeking peace;
> that we may see your face
> and be satisfied in you.
> through Jesus Christ, Amen.[1]

---

[1] Janet Morley, *All Desires Known*, p. 9.

SELECT BIBLIOGRAPHY

R. Bauckham, *The Theology of the Book of Revelation*, CUP 1993.

A. Boesak, *Comfort and Protest*, St Andrew Press 1987.

M. E. Boring, *The Book of Revelation* (Interpretation. A Bible Commentary for Teaching and Preaching), John Knox Press 1989.

B. E. Daley, *The Hope of the Early Church: A Handbook of Patristic Eschatology*, CUP 1991.

C. Hemer, *The Letters to the Seven Churches of Asia Minor in their Local Setting*, Sheffield Academic Press 1986.

C. Mesters, *Defenseless Flower*, Orbis Books 1989.

J. Morley, *All Desires Known*, enlarged ed., SPCK 1992.

O. O'Donovan, 'The Political Thought of the Book of Revelation', *Tyndale Bulletin* vol. 37, 1986.

C. Rowland, *The Open Heaven. A Study of Apocalyptic in Judaism and Early Christianity*, SPCK 1982.

G. E. M. de Ste Croix, *The Class Struggle in the Ancient Greek World from the Archaic Age to the Arab Conquests*, Duckworth 1982.

E. Schüssler-Fiorenza, *The Book of Revelation. Justice and Judgement*, SCM Press 1985.
—, *Revelation. Vision of a Just World* (Proclamation Commentary) Fortress Press 1991.

J. Sweet, *Revelation* (SCM Pelican Commentary), SCM Press 1979.

K. Wengst, *Pax Romana and the Peace of Jesus Christ*, SCM Press 1987.

W. Wink, *Engaging the Powers. Discernment and Resistance in a World of Domination*, Fortress Press 1992.